INVESTMENTS WORKBOOK

Principles of Portfolio and Equity Analysis

CFA Institute is the premier association for investment professionals around the world, with over 101,000 members in 134 countries. Since 1963 the organization has developed and administered the renowned Chartered Financial Analyst® Program. With a rich history of leading the investment profession, CFA Institute has set the highest standards in ethics, education, and professional excellence within the global investment community, and is the foremost authority on investment profession conduct and practice.

Each book in the CFA Institute Investment Series is geared toward industry practitioners along with graduate-level finance students and covers the most important topics in the industry. The authors of these cutting-edge books are themselves industry professionals and academics and bring their wealth of knowledge and expertise to this series.

INVESTMENTS WORKBOOK

Principles of Portfolio and Equity Analysis

Michael G. McMillan, CFA

Jerald E. Pinto, CFA

Wendy L. Pirie, CFA

Gerhard Van de Venter, CFA

WILEY

John Wiley & Sons, Inc.

Published by John Wiley & Sons, Inc., Hoboken, New Jersey.
Published simultaneously in Canada.

ISBN 978-0-470-91582-0 (paper); ISBN 978-1-118-00117-2 (ebk);
ISBN 978-1-118-00118-9 (ebk); ISBN 978-1-118-00119-6 (ebk)

10 9 8 7 6 5 4 3 2 1

CONTENTS

PART I

LEARNING OUTCOMES, SUMMARY OVERVIEW, AND PROBLEMS

CHAPTER 1

MARKET ORGANIZATION AND STRUCTURE

LEARNING OUTCOMES

After completing this chapter, you will be able to do the following:

- Explain and illustrate the main functions of the financial system.
- Describe classifications of assets and markets.
- Describe the major types of securities, currencies, contracts, commodities, and real assets that trade in organized markets, including their distinguishing characteristics and major subtypes.
- Describe the types of financial intermediaries and the services that they provide.
- Compare and contrast the positions an investor can take in an asset.
- Calculate and interpret the leverage ratio, the rate of return on a margin transaction, and the security price at which the investor would receive a margin call.
- Compare and contrast execution, validity, and clearing instructions.
- Compare and contrast market orders with limit orders.
- Describe the primary and secondary markets and explain how secondary markets support primary markets.
- Describe how securities, contracts, and currencies are traded in quote-driven markets, order-driven markets, and brokered markets.
- Describe the characteristics of a well-functioning financial system.
- Describe the objectives of market regulation.

SUMMARY OVERVIEW

- The financial system consists of mechanisms that allow strangers to contract with each other to move money through time, to hedge risks, and to exchange assets that they value less for those that they value more.
- Investors move money from the present to the future when they save. They expect a normal rate of return for bearing risk through time. Borrowers move money from the future to the present to fund current projects and expenditures. Hedgers trade to reduce their exposure to risks they prefer not to take. Information-motivated traders are active investment managers who try to indentify under- and overvalued instruments.

- Securities are first sold in primary markets by their issuers. They then trade in secondary markets.
- People invest in pooled investment vehicles to benefit from the investment management services of their managers.
- Forward contracts allow buyers and sellers to arrange for future sales at predetermined prices. Futures contracts are forward contracts guaranteed by clearinghouses. The guarantee ensures that strangers are willing to trade with each other and that traders can offset their positions by trading with anybody. These features of futures contract markets make them highly attractive to hedgers and information-motivated traders.
- Many financial intermediaries connect buyers to sellers in a given instrument, acting directly as brokers and exchanges or indirectly as dealers and arbitrageurs.
- Financial intermediaries create instruments when they conduct arbitrage, securitize assets, borrow to lend, manage investment funds, or pool insurance contracts. These activities all transform cash flows and risks from one form to another. Their services allow buyers and sellers to connect with each other through instruments that meet their specific needs.
- Financial markets work best when strangers can contract with each other without worrying about whether their counterparts are able and willing to honor their contract. Clearinghouses, variation margins, maintenance margins, and settlement guarantees made by creditworthy brokers on behalf of their clients help manage credit risk and ultimately allow strangers to contract with each other.
- Information-motivated traders short sell when they expect that prices will fall. Hedgers short sell to reduce the risks of a long position in a related contract or commodity.
- Margin loans allow people to buy more securities than their equity would otherwise permit them to buy. The larger positions expose them to more risk so that gains and losses for a given amount of equity will be larger. The leverage ratio is the value of a position divided by the value of the equity supporting it. The returns to the equity in a position are equal to the leverage ratio times the returns to the unleveraged position.
- To protect against credit losses, brokers demand maintenance margin payments from their customers who have borrowed cash or securities when adverse price changes cause their customer's equity to drop below the maintenance margin ratio. Brokers close positions for customers who do not satisfy these margin calls.
- Orders are instructions to trade. They always specify instrument, side (buy or sell), and quantity. They usually also provide several other instructions.
- Market orders tend to fill quickly but often at inferior prices. Limit orders generally fill at better prices if they fill, but they may not fill. Traders choose order submission strategies on the basis of how quickly they want to trade, the prices they are willing to accept, and the consequences of failing to trade.
- Stop instructions are attached to other orders to delay efforts to fill them until the stop condition is satisfied. Although stop orders are often used to stop losses, they are not always effective.
- Issuers sell their securities using underwritten public offerings, best efforts public offerings, private placements, shelf registrations, dividend reinvestment programs, and rights offerings. Investment banks have a conflict of interests when setting the initial offering price in an IPO.
- Well-functioning secondary markets are essential to raising capital in the primary markets because investors value the ability to sell their securities if they no longer want to hold them or if they need to disinvest to raise cash. If they cannot trade their securities in a liquid market, they will not pay as much for them.

- Matching buyers and sellers in call markets is easy because the traders (or their orders) come together at the same time and place.
- Dealers provide liquidity in quote-driven markets. Public traders as well as dealers provide liquidity in order-driven markets.
- Order-driven markets arrange trades by ranking orders using precedence rules. The rules generally ensure that traders who provide the best prices, display the most size, and arrive early trade first. Continuous order-driven markets price orders using the discriminatory pricing rule. Under this rule, standing limit orders determine trade prices.
- Brokers help people trade unique instruments or positions for which finding a buyer or a seller is difficult.
- Transaction costs are lower in transparent markets than in opaque markets because traders can more easily determine market value and more easily manage their trading in transparent markets.
- A well-functioning financial system allows people to trade instruments that best solve their wealth and risk management problems with low transaction costs. Complete and liquid markets characterize a well-functioning financial system. Complete markets are markets in which the instruments needed to solve investment and risk management problems are available to trade. Liquid markets are markets in which traders can trade when they want to trade at low cost.
- The financial system is operationally efficient when its markets are liquid. Liquid markets lower the costs of raising capital.
- A well-functioning financial system promotes wealth by ensuring that capital allocation decisions are well made. A well-functioning financial system also promotes wealth by allowing people to share the risks associated with valuable products that would otherwise not be undertaken.
- Prices are informationally efficient when they reflect all available information about fundamental values. Information-motivated traders make prices informationally efficient. Prices will be most informative in liquid markets because information-motivated traders will not invest in information and research if establishing positions based on their analyses is too costly.
- Regulators generally seek to promote fair and orderly markets in which traders can trade at prices that accurately reflect fundamental values without incurring excessive transaction costs. Governmental agencies and self-regulating organizations of practitioners provide regulatory services that attempt to make markets safer and more efficient.
- Mandated financial disclosure programs for the issuers of publicly traded securities ensure that information necessary to estimate security values is available to financial analysts on a consistent basis.

PROBLEMS

1. Akihiko Takabe has designed a sophisticated forecasting model, which predicts the movements in the overall stock market, in the hope of earning a return in excess of a fair return for the risk involved. He uses the predictions of the model to decide whether to buy, hold, or sell the shares of an index fund that aims to replicate the movements of the stock market. Takabe would *best* be characterized as a(n):

   A. Hedger.
   B. Investor.
   C. Information-motivated trader.

2. James Beach is young and has substantial wealth. A significant proportion of his stock portfolio consists of emerging market stocks that offer relatively high expected returns at the cost of relatively high risk. Beach believes that investment in emerging market stocks is appropriate for him given his ability and willingness to take risk. Which of the following labels *most appropriately* describes Beach?

   A. Hedger.
   B. Investor.
   C. Information-motivated trader.

3. Lisa Smith owns a manufacturing company in the United States. Her company has sold goods to a customer in Brazil and will be paid in Brazilian real (BRL) in three months. Smith is concerned about the possibility of the BRL depreciating more than expected against the U.S. dollar (USD). Therefore, she is planning to sell three-month futures contracts on the BRL. The seller of such contracts generally gains when the BRL depreciates against the USD. If Smith were to sell these future contracts, she would *most appropriately* be described as a(n):

   A. Hedger.
   B. Investor.
   C. Information-motivated trader.

4. Which of the following is *not* a function of the financial system?

   A. To regulate arbitrageurs' profits (excess returns).
   B. To help the economy achieve allocational efficiency.
   C. To facilitate borrowing by businesses to fund current operations.

5. An investor primarily invests in stocks of publicly traded companies. The investor wants to increase the diversification of his portfolio. A friend has recommended investing in real estate properties. The purchase of real estate would *best* be characterized as a transaction in the:

   A. Derivative investment market.
   B. Traditional investment market.
   C. Alternative investment market.

6. A hedge fund holds its excess cash in 90-day commercial paper and negotiable certificates of deposit. The cash management policy of the hedge fund is *best described* as using:

   A. Capital market instruments.
   B. Money market instruments.
   C. Intermediate-term debt instruments.

7. An oil and gas exploration and production company announces that it is offering 30 million shares to the public at $45.50 each. This transaction is *most likely* a sale in the:

   A. Futures market.
   B. Primary market.
   C. Secondary market.

8. Consider a mutual fund that invests primarily in fixed-income securities that have been determined to be appropriate given the fund's investment goal. Which of the following is *least likely* to be a part of this fund?

   A. Warrants.
   B. Commercial paper.
   C. Repurchase agreements.

9. A friend has asked you to explain the differences between open-end and closed-end funds. Which of the following will you *most likely* include in your explanation?

   A. Closed-end funds are unavailable to new investors.
   B. When investors sell the shares of an open-end fund, they can receive a discount or a premium to the fund's net asset value.
   C. When selling shares, investors in an open-end fund sell the shares back to the fund whereas investors in a closed-end fund sell the shares to others in the secondary market.

10. The usefulness of a forward contract is limited by some problems. Which of the following is *most likely* one of those problems?

    A. Once you have entered into a forward contract, it is difficult to exit from the contract.
    B. Entering into a forward contract requires the long party to deposit an initial amount with the short party.
    C. If the price of the underlying asset moves adversely from the perspective of the long party, periodic payments must be made to the short party.

11. Tony Harris is planning to start trading in commodities. He has heard about the use of futures contracts on commodities and is learning more about them. Which of the following is Harris *least likely* to find associated with a futures contract?

    A. Existence of counterparty risk.
    B. Standardized contractual terms.
    C. Payment of an initial margin to enter into a contract.

12. A German company that exports machinery is expecting to receive $10 million in three months. The firm converts all its foreign currency receipts into euros. The chief financial officer of the company wishes to lock in a minimum fixed rate for converting the $10 million to euro but also wants to keep the flexibility to use the future spot rate if it is favorable. What hedging transaction is *most likely* to achieve this objective?

    A. Selling dollars forward.
    B. Buying put options on the dollar.
    C. Selling futures contracts on dollars.

13. A book publisher requires substantial quantities of paper. The publisher and a paper producer have entered into an agreement for the publisher to buy and the producer to supply a given quantity of paper four months later at a price agreed upon today. This agreement is a:

    A. Futures contract.
    B. Forward contract.
    C. Commodity swap.

14. The Standard & Poor's Depositary Receipts (SPDRs) is an investment that tracks the S&P 500 stock market index. Purchases and sales of SPDRs during an average trading day are *best* described as:

    A. Primary market transactions in a pooled investment.
    B. Secondary market transactions in a pooled investment.
    C. Secondary market transactions in an actively managed investment.

15. The Standard & Poor's Depositary Receipts (SPDRs) is an exchange-traded fund in the United States that is designed to track the S&P 500 stock market index. The current price of a share of SPDRs is \$113. A trader has just bought call options on shares of SPDRs for a premium of \$3 per share. The call options expire in five months and have an exercise price of \$120 per share. On the expiration date, the trader will exercise the call options (ignore any transaction costs) if and only if the shares of SPDRs are trading:

    A. Below \$120 per share.
    B. Above \$120 per share.
    C. Above \$123 per share.

16. Which of the following statements about exchange-traded funds is *most correct*?

    A. Exchange-traded funds are not backed by any assets.
    B. The investment companies that create exchange-traded funds are financial intermediaries.
    C. The transaction costs of trading shares of exchange-traded funds are substantially greater than the combined costs of trading the underlying assets of the fund.

17. Jason Schmidt works for a hedge fund and he specializes in finding profit opportunities that are the result of inefficiencies in the market for convertible bonds—bonds that can be converted into a predetermined amount of a company's common stock. Schmidt tries to find convertibles that are priced inefficiently relative to the underlying stock. The trading strategy involves the simultaneous purchase of the convertible bond and the short sale of the underlying common stock. The above process could best be described as:

    A. Hedging.
    B. Arbitrage.
    C. Securitization.

18. Pierre-Louis Robert just purchased a call option on shares of the Michelin Group. A few days ago he wrote a put option on Michelin shares. The call and put options have the same exercise price, expiration date, and number of shares underlying. Considering both positions, Robert's exposure to the risk of the stock of the Michelin Group is:

    A. Long.
    B. Short.
    C. Neutral.

19. An online brokerage firm has set the minimum margin requirement at 55 percent. What is the maximum leverage ratio associated with a position financed by this minimum margin requirement?

    A. 1.55.
    B. 1.82.
    C. 2.22.

20. A trader has purchased 200 shares of a non-dividend-paying firm on margin at a price of $50 per share. The leverage ratio is 2.5. Six months later, the trader sells these shares at $60 per share. Ignoring the interest paid on the borrowed amount and the transaction costs, what was the return to the trader during the six-month period?

    A. 20 percent.
    B. 33.33 percent.
    C. 50 percent.

21. Jason Williams purchased 500 shares of a company at $32 per share. The stock was bought on 75 percent margin. One month later, Williams had to pay interest on the amount borrowed at a rate of 2 percent per month. At that time, Williams received a dividend of $0.50 per share. Immediately after that he sold the shares at $28 per share. He paid commissions of $10 on the purchase and $10 on the sale of the stock. What was the rate of return on this investment for the one-month period?

    A. −12.5 percent.
    B. −15.4 percent.
    C. −50.1 percent.

22. Caroline Rogers believes the price of Gamma Corp. stock will go down in the near future. She has decided to sell short 200 shares of Gamma Corp. at the current market price of €47. The initial margin requirement is 40 percent. Which of the following is an appropriate statement regarding the margin requirement that Rogers is subject to on this short sale?

    A. She will need to contribute €3,760 as margin.
    B. She will need to contribute €5,640 as margin.
    C. She will only need to leave the proceeds from the short sale as deposit and does not need to contribute any additional funds.

23. The current price of a stock is $25 per share. You have $10,000 to invest. You borrow an additional $10,000 from your broker and invest $20,000 in the stock. If the maintenance margin is 30 percent, at what price will a margin call first occur?

    A. $9.62.
    B. $17.86.
    C. $19.71.

24. You have placed a sell market-on-open order—a market order that would automatically be submitted at the market's open tomorrow and would fill at the market price. Your instruction, to sell the shares at the market open, is a(n):

    A. Execution instruction.
    B. Validity instruction.
    C. Clearing instruction.

25. A market has the following limit orders standing on its book for a particular stock. The bid and ask sizes are number of shares in hundreds.

Bid Size	Limit Price	Offer Size
5	€9.73	
12	€9.81	
4	€9.84	
6	€9.95	
	€10.02	5
	€10.10	12
	€10.14	8

What is the market?

A. 9.73 bid, offered at 10.14.
B. 9.81 bid, offered at 10.10.
C. 9.95 bid, offered at 10.02.

26. Consider the following limit order book for a stock. The bid and ask sizes are number of shares in hundreds.

Bid Size	Limit Price	Offer Size
3	¥122.80	
8	¥123.00	
4	¥123.35	
	¥123.80	7
	¥124.10	6
	¥124.50	7

A new buy limit order is placed for 300 shares at ¥123.40. This limit order is said to:

A. Take the market.
B. Make the market.
C. Make a new market.

27. Currently, the market in a stock is "$54.62 bid, offered at $54.71." A new sell limit order is placed at $54.62. This limit order is said to:

A. Take the market.
B. Make the market.
C. Make a new market.

28. Jim White has sold short 100 shares of Super Stores at a price of $42 per share. He has also simultaneously placed a "good-till-cancelled, stop 50, limit 55 buy" order. Assume that if the stop condition specified by White is satisfied and the order becomes valid, it will get executed. Excluding transaction costs, what is the maximum possible loss that White can have?

A. $800.
B. $1,300.
C. Unlimited.

29. You own shares of a company that are currently trading at $30 a share. Your technical analysis of the shares indicates a support level of $27.50. That is, if the price of the shares is

going down, it is more likely to stay above this level rather than fall below it. If the price does fall below this level, however, you believe that the price may continue to decline. You have no immediate intent to sell the shares but are concerned about the possibility of a huge loss if the share price declines below the support level. Which of the following types of orders could you place to most appropriately address your concern?

A. Short sell order.
B. Good-till-cancelled stop sell order.
C. Good-till-cancelled stop buy order.

30. In an underwritten offering, the risk that the entire issue may not be sold to the public at the stipulated offering price is borne by the:

A. Issuer.
B. Investment bank.
C. Buyers of the part of the issue that is sold.

31. A British company listed on the Alternative Investment Market of the London Stock Exchange, announced the sale of 6,686,665 shares to a small group of qualified investors at £0.025 per share. Which of the following *best describes* this sale?

A. Shelf registration.
B. Private placement.
C. Initial public offering.

32. A German publicly traded company, to raise new capital, gave its existing shareholders the opportunity to subscribe for new shares. The existing shareholders could purchase two new shares at a subscription price of €4.58 per share for every 15 shares held. This is an example of a(n):

A. Rights offering.
B. Private placement.
C. Initial public offering.

33. Consider an order-driven system that allows hidden orders. The following four sell orders on a particular stock are currently in the system's limit order book. Based on the commonly used order precedence hierarchy, which of these orders will have precedence over others?

Order Number	Time of Arrival (HH:MM:SS)	Limit Price	Special Instruction (If any)
I	9:52:01	€20.33	
II	9:52:08	€20.29	Hidden order
III	9:53:04	€20.29	
IV	9:53:49	€20.29	

A. Order I (time of arrival of 9:52:01).
B. Order II (time of arrival of 9:52:08).
C. Order III (time of arrival of 9:53:04).

34. Zhenhu Li has submitted an immediate-or-cancel buy order for 500 shares of a company at a limit price of CNY 74.25. There are two sell limit orders standing in that stock's

order book at that time. One is for 300 shares at a limit price of CNY 74.30 and the other is for 400 shares at a limit price of CNY 74.35. How many shares in Li's order would get cancelled?

A. None (the order would remain open but unfilled).
B. 200 (300 shares would get filled).
C. 500 (there would be no fill).

35. A market has the following limit orders standing on its book for a particular stock:

Buyer	Bid Size (number of shares)	Limit Price	Offer Size (number of shares)	Seller
Keith	1,000	£19.70		
Paul	200	£19.84		
Ann	400	£19.89		
Mary	300	£20.02		
		£20.03	800	Jack
		£20.11	1,100	Margaret
		£20.16	400	Jeff

Ian submits a day order to sell 1,000 shares, limit £19.83. Assuming that no more buy orders are submitted on that day after Ian submits his order, what would be Ian's average trade price?

A. £19.70.
B. £19.92.
C. £20.05.

36. A financial analyst is examining whether a country's financial market is well functioning. She finds that the transaction costs in this market are low and trading volumes are high. She concludes that the market is quite liquid. In such a market:

A. Traders will find it hard to make use of their information.
B. Traders will find it easy to trade and their trading will make the market less informationally efficient.
C. Traders will find it easy to trade and their trading will make the market more informationally efficient.

37. The government of a country whose financial markets are in an early stage of development has hired you as a consultant on financial market regulation. Your first task is to prepare a list of the objectives of market regulation. Which of the following is *least likely* to be included in this list of objectives?

A. Minimize agency problems in the financial markets.
B. Ensure that financial markets are fair and orderly.
C. Ensure that investors in the stock market achieve a rate of return that is at least equal to the risk-free rate of return.

CHAPTER 2

SECURITY MARKET INDICES

LEARNING OUTCOMES

After completing this chapter, you will be able to do the following:

- Describe a security market index.
- Calculate and interpret the value, price return, and total return of an index.
- Discuss the choices and issues in index construction and management.
- Compare and contrast the different weighting methods used in index construction.
- Calculate and interpret the value and return of an index on the basis of its weighting method.
- Discuss rebalancing and reconstitution.
- Discuss uses of security market indices.
- Discuss types of equity indices.
- Discuss types of fixed-income indices.
- Discuss indices representing alternative investments.
- Compare and contrast the types of security market indices.

SUMMARY OVERVIEW

- Security market indices are intended to measure the values of different target markets (security markets, market segments, or asset classes).
- The constituent securities selected for inclusion in the security market index are intended to represent the target market.
- A price return index reflects only the prices of the constituent securities.
- A total return index reflects not only the prices of the constituent securities but also the reinvestment of all income received since the inception of the index.
- Methods used to weight the constituents of an index range from the very simple, such as price and equal weightings, to the more complex, such as market-capitalization and fundamental weightings.
- Choices in index construction—in particular, the choice of weighting method—affect index valuation and returns.

- Index management includes (1) periodic rebalancing to ensure that the index maintains appropriate weightings and (2) reconstitution to ensure the index represents the desired target market.
- Rebalancing and reconstitution create turnover in an index. Reconstitution can dramatically affect prices of current and prospective constituents.
- Indices serve a variety of purposes. They gauge market sentiment and serve as benchmarks for actively managed portfolios. They act as proxies for measuring systematic risk and risk-adjusted performance. They also serve as proxies for asset classes in asset allocation models and as model portfolios for investment products.
- Investors can choose from security market indices representing various asset classes, including equity, fixed-income, commodity, real estate, and hedge fund indices.
- Within most asset classes, index providers offer a wide variety of indices, ranging from broad market indices to highly specialized indices based on the issuer's geographic region, economic development group, or economic sector or other factors.
- Proper use of security market indices depends on understanding their construction and management.

PROBLEMS

1. A security market index represents the:
   A. Risk of a security market.
   B. Security market as a whole.
   C. Security market, market segment, or asset class.

2. Security market indices are:
   A. Constructed and managed like a portfolio of securities.
   B. Simple interchangeable tools for measuring the returns of different asset classes.
   C. Valued on a regular basis using the actual market prices of the constituent securities.

3. When creating a security market index, an index provider must first determine the:
   A. Target market.
   B. Appropriate weighting method.
   C. Number of constituent securities.

4. One month after inception, the price return version and total return version of a single index (consisting of identical securities and weights) will be equal if:
   A. Market prices have not changed.
   B. Capital gains are offset by capital losses.
   C. The securities do not pay dividends or interest.

5. The values of a price return index and a total return index consisting of identical equal-weighted dividend-paying equities will be equal:
   A. Only at inception.
   B. At inception and on rebalancing dates.
   C. At inception and on reconstitution dates.

6. An analyst gathers the following information for an equal-weighted index comprised of assets Able, Baker, and Charlie:

Security	Beginning of Period Price (€)	End of Period Price (€)	Total Dividends (€)
Able	10.00	12.00	0.75
Baker	20.00	19.00	1.00
Charlie	30.00	30.00	2.00

The price return of the index is:

A. 1.7%.
B. 5.0%.
C. 11.4%.

7. An analyst gathers the following information for an equal-weighted index comprised of assets Able, Baker, and Charlie:

Security	Beginning of Period Price (€)	End of Period Price (€)	Total Dividends (€)
Able	10.00	12.00	0.75
Baker	20.00	19.00	1.00
Charlie	30.00	30.00	2.00

The total return of the index is:

A. 5.0%.
B. 7.9%.
C. 11.4%.

8. An analyst gathers the following information for a price-weighted index comprised of securities ABC, DEF, and GHI:

Security	Beginning of Period Price (£)	End of Period Price (£)	Total Dividends (£)
ABC	25.00	27.00	1.00
DEF	35.00	25.00	1.50
GHI	15.00	16.00	1.00

The price return of the index is:

A. −4.6%.
B. −9.3%.
C. −13.9%.

9. An analyst gathers the following information for a market-capitalization-weighted index comprised of securities MNO, QRS, and XYZ:

Security	Beginning of Period Price (¥)	End of Period Price (¥)	Dividends per Share (¥)	Shares Outstanding
MNO	2,500	2,700	100	5,000
QRS	3,500	2,500	150	7,500
XYZ	1,500	1,600	100	10,000

The price return of the index is:

A. −9.33%.
B. −10.23%.
C. −13.90%.

10. An analyst gathers the following information for a market-capitalization-weighted index comprised of securities MNO, QRS, and XYZ:

Security	Beginning of Period Price (¥)	End of Period Price (¥)	Dividends Per Share (¥)	Shares Outstanding
MNO	2,500	2,700	100	5,000
QRS	3,500	2,500	150	7,500
XYZ	1,500	1,600	100	10,000

The total return of the index is:

A. 1.04%.
B. −5.35%.
C. −10.23%.

11. When creating a security market index, the target market:

A. Determines the investment universe.
B. Is usually a broadly defined asset class.
C. Determines the number of securities to be included in the index.

12. An analyst gathers the following data for a price-weighted index:

	Beginning of Period		End of Period	
Security	Price (€)	Shares	Price (€)	Shares
A	20.00	300	22.00	300
B	50.00	300	48.00	300
C	26.00	2,000	30.00	2,000

The price return of the index over the period is:

A. 4.2%.
B. 7.1%.
C. 21.4%.

13. An analyst gathers the following data for a value-weighted index:

	Beginning of Period		End of Period	
Security	Price (£)	Shares	Price (£)	Shares
A	20.00	300	22.00	300
B	50.00	300	48.00	300
C	26.00	2,000	30.00	2,000

The return on the value-weighted index over the period is:

A. 7.1%.
B. 11.0%.
C. 21.4%.

14. An analyst gathers the following data for an equally-weighted index:

	Beginning of Period		End of Period	
Security	Price (¥)	Shares	Price (¥)	Shares
A	20.00	300	22.00	300
B	50.00	300	48.00	300
C	26.00	2,000	30.00	2,000

The return on the index over the period is:

A. 4.2%.
B. 6.8%.
C. 7.1%.

15. Which of the following index weighting methods requires an adjustment to the divisor after a stock split?

A. Price weighting.
B. Fundamental weighting.
C. Market-capitalization weighting.

16. If the price return of an equal-weighted index exceeds that of a market-capitalization-weighted index comprised of the same securities, the *most likely* explanation is:

A. Stock splits.
B. Dividend distributions.
C. Outperformance of small-market-capitalization stocks.

17. A float-adjusted market-capitalization-weighted index weights each of its constituent securities by its price and:

A. Its trading volume.
B. The number of its shares outstanding.
C. The number of its shares available to the investing public.

18. Which of the following index weighting methods is *most likely* subject to a value tilt?

A. Equal weighting.
B. Fundamental weighting.
C. Market-capitalization weighting.

19. Rebalancing an index is the process of periodically adjusting the constituent:
    A. Securities' weights to optimize investment performance.
    B. Securities to maintain consistency with the target market.
    C. Securities' weights to maintain consistency with the index's weighting method.

20. Which of the following index weighting methods requires the most frequent rebalancing?
    A. Price weighting.
    B. Equal weighting.
    C. Market-capitalization weighting.

21. Reconstitution of a security market index reduces:
    A. Portfolio turnover.
    B. The need for rebalancing.
    C. The likelihood that the index includes securities that are not representative of the target market.

22. Security market indices are used as:
    A. Measures of investment returns.
    B. Proxies to measure unsystematic risk.
    C. Proxies for specific asset classes in asset allocation models.

23. Uses of market indices do not include serving as a:
    A. Measure of systematic risk.
    B. Basis for new investment products.
    C. Benchmark for evaluating portfolio performance.

24. Which of the following statements regarding sector indices is *most* accurate? Sector indices:
    A. Track different economic sectors and cannot be aggregated to represent the equivalent of a broad market index.
    B. Provide a means to determine whether an active investment manager is more successful at stock selection or sector allocation.
    C. Apply a universally agreed-upon sector classification system to identify the constituent securities of specific economic sectors, such as consumer goods, energy, finance, health care.

25. Which of the following is an example of a style index? An index based on:
    A. Geography.
    B. Economic sector.
    C. Market capitalization.

26. Which of the following statements regarding fixed-income indices is *most* accurate?
    A. Liquidity issues make it difficult for investors to easily replicate fixed-income indices.
    B. Rebalancing and reconstitution are the only sources of turnover in fixed-income indices.
    C. Fixed-income indices representing the same target market hold similar numbers of bonds.

27. An aggregate fixed-income index:
    A. Is comprised of corporate and asset-backed securities.
    B. Represents the market of government-issued securities.
    C. Can be subdivided by market or economic sector to create more narrowly defined indices.

28. Fixed-income indices are *least likely* constructed on the basis of:
    A. Maturity.
    B. Type of issuer.
    C. Coupon frequency.

29. Commodity index values are based on:
    A. Futures contract prices.
    B. The market price of the specific commodity.
    C. The average market price of a basket of similar commodities.

30. Which of the following statements is *most* accurate?
    A. Commodity indices all share similar weighting methods.
    B. Commodity indices containing the same underlying commodities offer similar returns.
    C. The performance of commodity indices can be quite different from that of the underlying commodities.

31. Which of the following is *not* a real estate index category?
    A. Appraisal index.
    B. Initial sales index.
    C. Repeat sales index.

32. A unique feature of hedge fund indices is that they:
    A. Are frequently equal weighted.
    B. Are determined by the constituents of the index.
    C. Reflect the value of private rather than public investments.

33. The returns of hedge fund indices are *most likely*:
    A. Biased upward.
    B. Biased downward.
    C. Similar across different index providers.

34. In comparison to equity indices, the constituent securities of fixed-income indices are:
    A. More liquid.
    B. Easier to price.
    C. Drawn from a larger investment universe.

CHAPTER 3

MARKET EFFICIENCY

LEARNING OUTCOMES

After completing this chapter, you will be able to do the following:

- Discuss market efficiency and related concepts, including their importance to investment practitioners.
- Explain the factors affecting a market's efficiency.
- Distinguish between market value and intrinsic value.
- Compare and contrast the weak-form, semistrong-form, and strong-form market efficiency.
- Explain the implications of each form of market efficiency for fundamental analysis, technical analysis, and the choice between active and passive portfolio management.
- Discuss identified market pricing anomalies and explain possible inconsistencies with market efficiency.
- Compare and contrast the behavioral finance view of investor behavior with that of traditional finance in regards to market efficiency.

SUMMARY OVERVIEW

- The efficiency of a market is affected by the number of market participants and depth of analyst coverage, information availability, and limits to trading.
- There are three forms of efficient markets, each based on what is considered to be the information used in determining asset prices. In the weak form, asset prices fully reflect all market data, which refers to all past price and trading volume information. In the semistrong form, asset prices reflect all publicly known and available information. In the strong form, asset prices fully reflect all information, which includes both public and private information.
- Intrinsic value refers to the true value of an asset, whereas market value refers to the price at which an asset can be bought or sold. When markets are efficient, the two should be the same or very close. But when markets are not efficient, the two can diverge significantly.
- Most empirical evidence supports the idea that securities markets in developed countries are semistrong-form efficient; however, empirical evidence does not support the strong form of the efficient market hypothesis.
- A number of anomalies have been documented that contradict the notion of market efficiency, including the size anomaly, the January anomaly, and the winners–losers anomalies. In most cases, however, contradictory evidence both supports and refutes the anomaly.

- Behavioral finance uses human psychology, such as cognitive biases, in an attempt to explain investment decisions. Whereas behavioral finance is helpful in understanding observed decisions, a market can still be considered efficient even if market participants exhibit seemingly irrational behaviors, such as herding.

PROBLEMS

1. In an efficient market, the change in a company's share price is *most likely* the result of:
   A. Insiders' private information.
   B. The previous day's change in stock price.
   C. New information coming into the market.
2. Regulation that restricts some investors from participating in a market will *most likely*:
   A. Impede market efficiency.
   B. Not affect market efficiency.
   C. Contribute to market efficiency.
3. With respect to efficient market theory, when a market allows short selling, the efficiency of the market is *most likely* to:
   A. Increase.
   B. Decrease.
   C. Remain the same.
4. Which of the following regulations will *most likely* contribute to market efficiency? Regulatory restrictions on:
   A. Short selling.
   B. Foreign traders.
   C. Insiders trading with nonpublic information.
5. Which of the following market regulations will *most likely* impede market efficiency?
   A. Restricting traders' ability to short sell.
   B. Allowing unrestricted foreign investor trading.
   C. Penalizing investors who trade with nonpublic information.
6. If markets are efficient, the difference between the intrinsic value and market value of a company's security is:
   A. Negative.
   B. Zero.
   C. Positive.
7. The intrinsic value of an undervalued asset is:
   A. Less than the asset's market value.
   B. Greater than the asset's market value.
   C. The value at which the asset can currently be bought or sold.
8. The market value of an undervalued asset is:
   A. Greater than the asset's intrinsic value.
   B. The value at which the asset can currently be bought or sold.
   C. Equal to the present value of all the asset's expected cash flows.

9. With respect to the efficient market hypothesis, if security prices reflect *only* past prices and trading volume information, then the market is:

    A. Weak-form efficient.
    B. Strong-form efficient.
    C. Semistrong-form efficient.

10. Which one of the following statements *best* describes the semistrong form of market efficiency?

    A. Empirical tests examine the historical patterns in security prices.
    B. Security prices reflect all publicly known and available information.
    C. Semistrong-form efficient markets are not necessarily weak-form efficient.

11. If markets are semistrong efficient, standard fundamental analysis will yield abnormal trading profits that are:

    A. Negative.
    B. Equal to zero.
    C. Positive.

12. If prices reflect all public and private information, the market is *best* described as:

    A. Weak-form efficient.
    B. Strong-form efficient.
    C. Semistrong-form efficient.

13. If markets are semistrong-form efficient, then passive portfolio management strategies are *most likely* to:

    A. Earn abnormal returns.
    B. Outperform active trading strategies.
    C. Underperform active trading strategies.

14. If a market is semistrong-form efficient, the risk-adjusted returns of a passively managed portfolio relative to an actively managed portfolio are *most likely*:

    A. Lower.
    B. Higher.
    C. The same.

15. Technical analysts assume that markets are:

    A. Weak-form efficient.
    B. Weak-form inefficient.
    C. Semistrong-form efficient.

16. Fundamental analysts assume that markets are:

    A. Weak-form inefficient.
    B. Semistrong-form efficient.
    C. Semistrong-form inefficient.

17. If a market is weak-form efficient but semistrong-form inefficient, then which of the following types of portfolio management is *most likely* to produce abnormal returns?

    A. Passive portfolio management.
    B. Active portfolio management based on technical analysis.
    C. Active portfolio management based on fundamental analysis.

18. An increase in the time between when an order to trade a security is placed and when the order is executed *most likely* indicates that market efficiency has:

    A. Decreased.
    B. Remained the same.
    C. Increased.

19. With respect to efficient markets, a company whose share price reacts gradually to the public release of its annual report *most likely* indicates that the market where the company trades is:

    A. Semistrong-form efficient.
    B. Subject to behavioral biases.
    C. Receiving additional information about the company.

20. Which of the following is *least likely* to explain the January effect anomaly?

    A. Tax-loss selling.
    B. Release of new information in January.
    C. Window dressing of portfolio holdings.

21. If a researcher conducting empirical tests of a trading strategy using time series of returns finds statistically significant abnormal returns, then the researcher has *most likely* found:

    A. A market anomaly.
    B. Evidence of market inefficiency.
    C. A strategy to produce future abnormal returns.

22. Which of the following market anomalies is inconsistent with weak-form market efficiency?

    A. Earnings surprise.
    B. Momentum pattern.
    C. Closed-end fund discount.

23. Researchers have found that value stocks have consistently outperformed growth stocks. An investor wishing to exploit the value effect should purchase the stock of companies with above-average:

    A. Dividend yields.
    B. Market-to-book ratios.
    C. Price-to-earnings ratios.

24. With respect to rational and irrational investment decisions, the efficient market hypothesis requires:

    A. Only that the market is rational.
    B. That all investors make rational decisions.
    C. That some investors make irrational decisions.

25. Observed overreactions in markets can be explained by an investor's degree of:

    A. Risk aversion.
    B. Loss aversion.
    C. Confidence in the market.

26. Like traditional finance models, the behavioral theory of loss aversion assumes that investors dislike risk; however, the dislike of risk in behavioral theory is assumed to be:

    A. Leptokurtic.
    B. Symmetrical.
    C. Asymmetrical.

CHAPTER 4

PORTFOLIO MANAGEMENT: AN OVERVIEW

LEARNING OUTCOMES

After completing this chapter, you will be able to do the following:

- Explain the importance of the portfolio perspective.
- Discuss the types of investment management clients and the distinctive characteristics and needs of each.
- Describe the steps in the portfolio management process.
- Describe, compare, and contrast mutual funds and other forms of pooled investments.

SUMMARY OVERVIEW

- In this chapter we have discussed how a portfolio approach to investing could be preferable to simply investing in individual securities.
- The problem with focusing on individual securities is that this approach may lead to the investor "putting all her eggs in one basket."
- Portfolios provide important diversification benefits, allowing risk to be reduced without necessarily affecting or compromising return.
- We have outlined the differing investment needs of various types of individual and institutional investors. Institutional clients include defined benefit pension plans, endowments and foundations, banks, insurance companies, investment companies, and sovereign wealth funds.
- Understanding the needs of your client and creating an investment policy statement represent the first steps of the portfolio management process. Those steps are followed by security analysis, portfolio construction, monitoring, and performance measurement stages.
- We also discussed the different types of investment products that investors can use to create their portfolio. These range from mutual funds, to exchange-traded funds, to hedge funds, to private equity funds.

PROBLEMS[1]

1. Investors should use a portfolio approach to:

   A. Reduce risk.
   B. Monitor risk.
   C. Eliminate risk.

2. Which of the following is the *best* reason for an investor to be concerned with the composition of a portfolio?

   A. Risk reduction.
   B. Downside risk protection.
   C. Avoidance of investment disasters.

3. With respect to the formation of portfolios, which of the following statements is most *accurate*?

   A. Portfolios affect risk less than returns.
   B. Portfolios affect risk more than returns.
   C. Portfolios affect risk and returns equally.

4. Which of the following institutions will *on average* have the greatest need for liquidity?

   A. Banks.
   B. Investment companies.
   C. Non-life insurance companies.

5. Which of the following institutional investors will *most likely* have the longest time horizon?

   A. Defined benefit plan.
   B. University endowment.
   C. Life insurance company.

6. A defined benefit plan with a large number of retirees is *likely* to have a high need for:

   A. Income.
   B. Liquidity.
   C. Insurance.

7. Which of the following institutional investors is *most likely* to manage investments in mutual funds?

   A. Insurance companies.
   B. Investment companies.
   C. University endowments.

8. With respect to the portfolio management process, the asset allocation is determined in the:

   A. Planning step.
   B. Feedback step.
   C. Execution step.

---

[1]These practice questions were developed by Stephen P. Huffman, CFA (University of Wisconsin, Oshkosh).

9. The planning step of the portfolio management process is *least likely* to include an assessment of the client's:

   A. Securities.
   B. Constraints.
   C. Risk tolerance.

10. With respect to the portfolio management process, the rebalancing of a portfolio's composition is *most likely* to occur in the:

    A. Planning step.
    B. Feedback step.
    C. Execution step.

11. An analyst gathers the following information for the asset allocations of three portfolios:

Portfolio	Fixed Income	Equity	Alternative Assets
1	25%	60%	15%
2	60%	25%	15%
3	15%	60%	25%

    Which of the portfolios is *most likely* appropriate for a client who has a high degree of risk tolerance?

    A. Portfolio 1.
    B. Portfolio 2.
    C. Portfolio 3.

12. Which of the following investment products is *most likely* to trade at their net asset value per share?

    A. Exchange-traded funds.
    B. Open-end mutual funds.
    C. Closed-end mutual funds.

13. Which of the following financial products is *least likely* to have a capital gain distribution?

    A. Exchange-traded funds.
    B. Open-end mutual funds.
    C. Closed-end mutual funds.

14. Which of the following forms of pooled investments is subject to the least amount of regulation?

    A. Hedge funds.
    B. Exchange-traded funds.
    C. Closed-end mutual funds.

15. Which of the following pooled investments is *most likely* characterized by a few large investments?

    A. Hedge funds.
    B. Buyout funds.
    C. Venture capital funds.

CHAPTER 5

PORTFOLIO RISK AND RETURN: PART I

LEARNING OUTCOMES

After completing this chapter, you will be able to do the following:

- Calculate and interpret major return measures and describe their applicability.
- Describe the characteristics of the major asset classes that investors would consider in forming portfolios according to mean–variance portfolio theory.
- Calculate and interpret the mean, variance, and covariance (or correlation) of asset returns based on historical data.
- Explain risk aversion and its implications for portfolio selection.
- Calculate and interpret portfolio standard deviation.
- Describe the effect on a portfolio's risk of investing in assets that are less than perfectly correlated.
- Describe and interpret the minimum-variance and efficient frontiers of risky assets and the global minimum-variance portfolio.
- Discuss the selection of an optimal portfolio, given an investor's utility (or risk aversion) and the capital allocation line.

SUMMARY OVERVIEW

- Holding period return is most appropriate for a single, predefined holding period.
- Multiperiod returns can be aggregated in many ways. Each return computation has special applications for evaluating investments.
- Risk-averse investors make investment decisions based on the risk–return trade-off, maximizing return for the same risk, and minimizing risk for the same return. They may be concerned, however, by deviations from a normal return distribution and from assumptions of financial markets' operational efficiency.
- Investors are risk averse, and historical data confirm that financial markets price assets for risk-averse investors.
- The risk of a two-asset portfolio is dependent on the proportions of each asset, their standard deviations and the correlation (or covariance) between the asset's returns. As the number of assets in a portfolio increases the correlation among asset risks becomes a more important determinate of portfolio risk.

- Combining assets with low correlations reduces portfolio risk.
- The two-fund separation theorem allows us to separate decision making into two steps. In the first step, the optimal risky portfolio and the capital allocation line are identified, which are the same for all investors. In the second step, investor risk preferences enable us to find a unique optimal investor portfolio for each investor.
- The addition of a risk-free asset creates portfolios that are dominant to portfolios of risky assets in all cases except for the optimal risky portfolio.

PROBLEMS[1]

1. An investor purchased 100 shares of a stock for $34.50 per share at the beginning of the quarter. If the investor sold all of the shares for $30.50 per share after receiving a $51.55 dividend payment at the end of the quarter, the holding period return is *closest* to:

   A. −13.0%.
   B. −11.6%.
   C. −10.1%.

2. An analyst obtains the following annual rates of return for a mutual fund:

Year	Return
2008	14%
2009	−10%
2010	−2%

   The fund's holding period return over the three-year period is *closest* to:

   A. 0.18%.
   B. 0.55%.
   C. 0.67%.

3. An analyst observes the following annual rates of return for a hedge fund:

Year	Return
2008	22%
2009	−25%
2010	11%

   The hedge fund's annual geometric mean return is *closest* to:

   A. 0.52%.
   B. 1.02%.
   C. 2.67%.

[1]These practice questions were developed by Stephen P. Huffman, CFA (University of Wisconsin, Oshkosh).

4. Which of the following return calculating methods is *best* for evaluating the annualized returns of a buy-and-hold strategy of an investor who has made annual deposits to an account for each of the last five years?

   A. Geometric mean return.
   B. Arithmetic mean return.
   C. Money-weighted return.

5. An investor evaluating the returns of three recently formed exchange-traded funds gathers the following information:

ETF	Time since Inception	Return since Inception
1	146 days	4.61%
2	5 weeks	1.10%
3	15 months	14.35%

   The ETF with the highest annualized rate of return is:

   A. ETF 1.
   B. ETF 2.
   C. ETF 3.

6. With respect to capital market theory, which of the following asset characteristics is *least likely* to impact the variance of an investor's equally weighted portfolio?

   A. Return on the asset.
   B. Standard deviation of the asset.
   C. Covariances of the asset with the other assets in the portfolio.

7. A portfolio manager creates the following portfolio:

Security	Security Weight	Expected Standard Deviation
1	30%	20%
2	70%	12%

   If the correlation of returns between the two securities is 0.40, the expected standard deviation of the portfolio is *closest* to:

   A. 10.7%.
   B. 11.3%.
   C. 12.1%.

8. A portfolio manager creates the following portfolio:

Security	Security Weight	Expected Standard Deviation
1	30%	20%
2	70%	12%

If the covariance of returns between the two securities is −0.0240, the expected standard deviation of the portfolio is *closest* to:

A. 2.4%.
B. 7.5%.
C. 9.2%.

Use the following data to answer Questions 9 and 10.

A portfolio manager creates the following portfolio:

Security	Security Weight	Expected Standard Deviation
1	30%	20%
2	70%	12%

9. If the standard deviation of the portfolio is 14.40%, the correlation between the two securities is equal to:

A. −1.0.
B. 0.0.
C. 1.0.

10. If the standard deviation of the portfolio is 14.40%, the covariance between the two securities is equal to:

A. 0.0006.
B. 0.0240.
C. 1.0000.

Use the following data to answer Questions 11 through 14.

An analyst observes the following historic geometric returns:

Asset Class	Geometric Return
Equities	8.0%
Corporate Bonds	6.5%
Treasury Bills	2.5%
Inflation	2.1%

11. The real rate of return for equities is *closest* to:

A. 5.4%.
B. 5.8%.
C. 5.9%.

12. The real rate of return for corporate bonds is *closest* to:

A. 4.3%.
B. 4.4%.
C. 4.5%.

13. The risk premium for equities is *closest* to:

A. 5.4%.
B. 5.5%.
C. 5.6%.

14. The risk premium for corporate bonds is *closest* to:

A. 3.5%.
B. 3.9%.
C. 4.0%.

15. With respect to trading costs, liquidity is *least likely* to impact the:

A. Stock price.
B. Bid-ask spreads.
C. Brokerage commissions.

16. Evidence of risk aversion is *best* illustrated by a risk-return relationship that is:

A. Negative.
B. Neutral.
C. Positive.

17. With respect to risk-averse investors, a risk-free asset will generate a numerical utility that is:

A. The same for all individuals.
B. Positive for risk-averse investors.
C. Equal to zero for risk seeking investors.

18. With respect to utility theory, the most risk-averse investor will have an indifference curve with the:

A. Most convexity.
B. Smallest intercept value.
C. Greatest slope coefficient.

19. With respect to an investor's utility function expressed as $U = E(r) - \frac{1}{2}A\sigma^2$, which of the following values for the measure for risk aversion has the *least* amount of risk-aversion?

A. −4
B. 0
C. 4

Use the following data to answer Questions 20 through 23.

A financial planner has created the following data to illustrate the application of utility theory to portfolio selection:

Investment	Expected Return	Expected Standard Deviation
1	18%	2%
2	19%	8%
3	20%	15%
4	18%	30%

20. A risk-neutral investor is *most likely* to choose:

    A. Investment 1.
    B. Investment 2.
    C. Investment 3.

21. If an investor's utility function is expressed as $U = E(r) - \frac{1}{2}A\sigma^2$ and the measure for risk aversion has a value of −2, the risk-seeking investor is *most likely* to choose:

    A. Investment 2.
    B. Investment 3.
    C. Investment 4.

22. If an investor's utility function is expressed as $U = E(r) - \frac{1}{2}A\sigma^2$ and the measure for risk aversion has a value of 2, the risk-averse investor is *most likely* to choose:

    A. Investment 1.
    B. Investment 2.
    C. Investment 3.

23. If an investor's utility function is expressed as $U = E(r) - \frac{1}{2}A\sigma^2$ and the measure for risk aversion has a value of 4, the risk-averse investor is *most likely* to choose:

    A. Investment 1.
    B. Investment 2.
    C. Investment 3.

24. With respect to the mean-variance portfolio theory, the capital allocation line, CAL, is the combination of the risk-free asset and a portfolio of all:

    A. Risky assets.
    B. Equity securities.
    C. Feasible investments.

25. Two individual investors with different levels of risk aversion will have optimal portfolios that are:

    A. Below the capital allocation line.
    B. On the capital allocation line.
    C. Above the capital allocation line.

Use the following data to answer Questions 26 through 28.

A portfolio manager creates the following portfolio:

Security	Expected Annual Return	Expected Standard Deviation
1	16%	20%
2	12%	20%

26. If the portfolio of the two securities has an expected return of 15%, the proportion invested in security 1 is:

A. 25%.
B. 50%.
C. 75%.

27. If the correlation of returns between the two securities is −0.15, the expected standard deviation of an equal-weighted portfolio is *closest* to:

A. 13.04%.
B. 13.60%.
C. 13.87%.

28. If the two securities are uncorrelated, the expected standard deviation of an equal-weighted portfolio is *closest* to:

A. 14.00%.
B. 14.14%.
C. 20.00%.

29. As the number of assets in an equally weighted portfolio increases, the contribution of each individual asset's variance to the volatility of the portfolio:

A. Increases.
B. Decreases.
C. Remains the same.

30. With respect to an equally weighted portfolio made up of a large number of assets, which of the following contributes the *most* to the volatility of the portfolio?

A. Average variance of the individual assets.
B. Standard deviation of the individual assets.
C. Average covariance between all pairs of assets.

31. The correlation between assets in a two-asset portfolio increases during a market decline. If there is no change in the proportion of each asset held in the portfolio or the expected standard deviation of the individual assets, the volatility of the portfolio is *most likely* to:

A. Increase.
B. Decrease.
C. Remain the same.

Use the following data to answer Questions 32 through 34.

An analyst has made the following return projections for each of three possible outcomes with an equal likelihood of occurrence:

Asset	Outcome 1	Outcome 2	Outcome 3	Expected Return
1	12%	0%	6%	6%
2	12%	6%	0%	6%
3	0%	6%	12%	6%

32. Which pair of assets is perfectly negatively correlated?

A. Asset 1 and Asset 2.
B. Asset 1 and Asset 3.
C. Asset 2 and Asset 3.

33. If the analyst constructs two-asset portfolios that are equally weighted, which pair of assets has the *lowest* expected standard deviation?

    A. Asset 1 and Asset 2.
    B. Asset 1 and Asset 3.
    C. Asset 2 and Asset 3.

34. If the analyst constructs two-asset portfolios that are equally weighted, which pair of assets provides the *least* amount of risk reduction?

    A. Asset 1 and Asset 2.
    B. Asset 1 and Asset 3.
    C. Asset 2 and Asset 3.

35. Which of the following statements is *least* accurate? The efficient frontier is the set of all attainable risky assets with the:

    A. Highest expected return for a given level of risk.
    B. Lowest amount of risk for a given level of return.
    C. Highest expected return relative to the risk-free rate.

36. The portfolio on the minimum-variance frontier with the lowest standard deviation is:

    A. Unattainable.
    B. The optimal risky portfolio.
    C. The global minimum-variance portfolio.

37. The set of portfolios on the minimum-variance frontier that dominates all sets of portfolios below the global minimum-variance portfolio is the:

    A. Capital allocation line.
    B. Markowitz efficient frontier.
    C. Set of optimal risky portfolios.

38. The dominant capital allocation line is the combination of the risk-free asset and the:

    A. Optimal risky portfolio.
    B. Levered portfolio of risky assets.
    C. Global minimum-variance portfolio.

39. Compared to the efficient frontier of risky assets, the dominant capital allocation line has higher rates of return for levels of risk greater than the optimal risky portfolio because of the investor's ability to:

    A. Lend at the risk-free rate.
    B. Borrow at the risk-free rate.
    C. Purchase the risk-free asset.

40. With respect to the mean-variance theory, the optimal portfolio is determined by each individual investor's:

    A. Risk-free rate.
    B. Borrowing rate.
    C. Risk preference.

CHAPTER 6

PORTFOLIO RISK AND RETURN: PART II

LEARNING OUTCOMES

After completing this chapter, you will be able to do the following:

- Discuss the implications of combining a risk-free asset with a portfolio of risky assets.
- Explain and interpret the capital allocation line (CAL) and the capital market line (CML).
- Explain systematic and nonsystematic risk and why an investor should not expect to receive additional return for bearing nonsystematic risk.
- Explain return-generating models (including the market model) and their uses.
- Calculate and interpret beta.
- Explain the capital asset pricing model (CAPM) including the required assumptions, and the security market line (SML).
- Calculate and interpret the expected return of an asset using the CAPM.
- Illustrate applications of the CAPM and the SML.

SUMMARY OVERVIEW

- The capital market line is a special case of the capital allocation line, where the efficient portfolio is the market portfolio.
- Obtaining a unique optimal risky portfolio is not possible if investors are permitted to have heterogeneous beliefs because such beliefs will result in heterogeneous asset prices.
- Investors can leverage their portfolios by borrowing money and investing in the market.
- Systematic risk is the risk that affects the entire market or economy and is not diversifiable.
- Nonsystematic risk is local and can be diversified away by combining assets with low correlations.
- Beta risk, or systematic risk, is priced and earns a return, whereas nonsystematic risk is not priced.
- The expected return of an asset depends on its beta risk and can be computed using the CAPM, which is given by $E(R_i) = R_f + \beta_i[E(R_m) - R_f]$.
- The security market line is an implementation of the CAPM and applies to all securities, whether they are efficient or not.
- Expected return from the CAPM can be used for making capital budgeting decisions.

- Portfolios can be evaluated by several CAPM-based measures, such as the Sharpe ratio, the Treynor ratio, M^2, and Jensen's alpha.
- The SML can assist in security selection and optimal portfolio construction.

PROBLEMS[1]

1. The line depicting the risk and return of portfolio combinations of a risk-free asset and any risky asset is the:

   A. Security market line.
   B. Capital allocation line.
   C. Security characteristic line.

2. The portfolio of a risk-free asset and a risky asset has a better risk–return tradeoff than investing in only one asset type because the correlation between the risk-free asset and the risky asset is equal to:

   A. −1.0.
   B. 0.0.
   C. 1.0.

3. With respect to capital market theory, an investor's optimal portfolio is the combination of a risk-free asset and a risky asset with the highest:

   A. Expected return.
   B. Indifference curve.
   C. Capital allocation line slope.

4. Highly risk-averse investors will *most likely* invest the majority of their wealth in:

   A. Risky assets.
   B. Risk-free assets.
   C. The optimal risky portfolio.

5. The capital market line, CML, is the graph of the risk and return of portfolio combinations consisting of the risk-free asset and:

   A. Any risky portfolio.
   B. The market portfolio.
   C. The leveraged portfolio.

6. Which of the following statements *most accurately* defines the market portfolio in capital market theory? The market portfolio consists of all:

   A. Risky assets.
   B. Tradable assets.
   C. Investable assets.

7. With respect to capital market theory, the optimal risky portfolio:

   A. Is the market portfolio.
   B. Has the highest expected return.
   C. Has the lowest expected variance.

[1]Practice questions were developed by Stephen P. Huffman, CFA (University of Wisconsin, Oshkosh).

8. Relative to portfolios on the CML, any portfolio that plots above the CML is considered:
   A. Inferior.
   B. Inefficient.
   C. Unachievable.

9. A portfolio on the capital market line with returns greater than the returns on the market portfolio represents a(n):
   A. Lending portfolio.
   B. Borrowing portfolio.
   C. Unachievable portfolio.

10. With respect to the capital market line, a portfolio on the CML with returns less than the returns on the market portfolio represents a(n):
    A. Lending portfolio.
    B. Borrowing portfolio.
    C. Unachievable portfolio.

11. Which of the following types of risk is *most likely* avoided by forming a diversified portfolio?
    A. Total risk.
    B. Systematic risk.
    C. Nonsystematic risk.

12. Which of the following events is *most likely* an example of nonsystematic risk?
    A. A decline in interest rates.
    B. The resignation of chief executive officer.
    C. An increase in the value of the U.S. dollar.

13. With respect to the pricing of risk in capital market theory, which of the following statements is *most accurate*?
    A. All risk is priced.
    B. Systematic risk is priced.
    C. Nonsystematic risk is priced.

14. The sum of an asset's systematic variance and its nonsystematic variance of returns is equal to the asset's:
    A. Beta.
    B. Total risk.
    C. Total variance.

15. With respect to return-generating models, the intercept term of the market model is the asset's estimated:
    A. Beta.
    B. Alpha.
    C. Variance.

16. With respect to return-generating models, the slope term of the market model is an estimate of the asset's:
    A. Total risk.
    B. Systematic risk.
    C. Nonsystematic risk.

17. With respect to return-generating models, which of the following statements is *most accurate*? Return-generating models are used to directly estimate the:

    A. Expected return of a security.
    B. Weights of securities in a portfolio.
    C. Parameters of the capital market line.

Use the following data to answer questions 18 through 20:

An analyst gathers the following information:

Security	Expected Annual Return	Expected Standard Deviation	Correlation between Security and the Market
Security 1	11%	25%	0.6
Security 2	11%	20%	0.7
Security 3	14%	20%	0.8
Market	10%	15%	1.0

18. Which security has the *highest* total risk?

    A. Security 1.
    B. Security 2.
    C. Security 3.

19. Which security has the *highest* beta measure?

    A. Security 1.
    B. Security 2.
    C. Security 3.

20. Which security has the *least* amount of market risk?

    A. Security 1.
    B. Security 2.
    C. Security 3.

21. With respect to capital market theory, the average beta of all assets in the market is:

    A. Less than 1.0.
    B. Equal to 1.0.
    C. Greater than 1.0.

22. The slope of the security characteristic line is an asset's:

    A. Beta.
    B. Excess return.
    C. Risk premium.

23. The graph of the capital asset pricing model is the:

    A. Capital market line.
    B. Security market line.
    C. Security characteristic line.

24. With respect to capital market theory, correctly priced individual assets can be plotted on the:

    A. Capital market line.
    B. Security market line.
    C. Capital allocation line.

25. With respect to the capital asset pricing model, the primary determinant of expected return of an individual asset is the:

    A. Asset's beta.
    B. Market risk premium.
    C. Asset's standard deviation.

26. With respect to the capital asset pricing model, which of the following values of beta for an asset is *most likely* to have an expected return for the asset that is less than the risk-free rate?

    A. −0.5.
    B. 0.0.
    C. 0.5.

27. With respect to the capital asset pricing model, the market risk premium is:

    A. Less than the excess market return.
    B. Equal to the excess market return.
    C. Greater than the excess market return.

Use the following data to answer questions 28 through 31:

An analyst gathers the following information:

Security	Expected Standard Deviation	Beta
Security 1	25%	1.50
Security 2	15%	1.40
Security 3	20%	1.60

28. With respect to the capital asset pricing model, if the expected market risk premium is 6% and the risk-free rate is 3%, the expected return for Security 1 is *closest* to:

    A. 9.0%.
    B. 12.0%.
    C. 13.5%.

29. With respect to the capital asset pricing model, if expected return for Security 2 is equal to 11.4% and the risk-free rate is 3%, the expected return for the market is *closest* to:

    A. 8.4%.
    B. 9.0%.
    C. 10.3%.

30. With respect to the capital asset pricing model, if the expected market risk premium is 6% the security with the *highest* expected return is:
    A. Security 1.
    B. Security 2.
    C. Security 3.
31. With respect to the capital asset pricing model, a decline in the expected market return will have the *greatest* impact on the expected return of:
    A. Security 1.
    B. Security 2.
    C. Security 3.
32. Which of the following performance measures is consistent with the CAPM?
    A. *M*-squared.
    B. Sharpe ratio.
    C. Jensen's alpha.
33. Which of the following performance measures does *not* require the measure to be compared to another value?
    A. Sharpe ratio.
    B. Treynor ratio.
    C. Jensen's alpha.
34. Which of the following performance measures is *most* appropriate for an investor who is *not* fully diversified?
    A. *M*-squared.
    B. Treynor ratio.
    C. Jensen's alpha.
35. Analysts who have estimated returns of an asset to be greater than the expected returns generated by the capital asset pricing model should consider the asset to be:
    A. Overvalued.
    B. Undervalued.
    C. Properly valued.
36. With respect to capital market theory, which of the following statements *best* describes the effect of the homogeneity assumption? Because all investors have the same economic expectations of future cash flows for all assets, investors will invest in:
    A. The same optimal risky portfolio.
    B. The S&P 500 Index.
    C. Assets with the same amount of risk.
37. With respect to capital market theory, which of the following assumptions allows for the existence of the market portfolio? All investors:
    A. Are price takers.
    B. Have homogeneous expectations.
    C. Plan for the same, single holding period.

38. The intercept of the best fit line formed by plotting the excess returns of a manager's portfolio on the excess returns of the market is *best* described as Jensen's:

    A. Beta.
    B. Ratio.
    C. Alpha.

39. Portfolio managers who are maximizing risk-adjusted returns will seek to invest *more* in securities with:

    A. Lower values of Jensen's alpha.
    B. Values of Jensen's alpha equal to 0.
    C. Higher values of Jensen's alpha.

40. Portfolio managers, who are maximizing risk-adjusted returns, will seek to invest *less* in securities with:

    A. Lower values for nonsystematic variance.
    B. Values of nonsystematic variance equal to 0.
    C. Higher values for nonsystematic variance.

CHAPTER 7

BASICS OF PORTFOLIO PLANNING AND CONSTRUCTION

LEARNING OUTCOMES

After completing this chapter, you will be able to do the following:

- Explain the reasons for a written investment policy statement (IPS).
- List and explain the major components of an IPS.
- Discuss risk and return objectives, including their preparation.
- Distinguish between the willingness and the ability (capacity) to take risk in analyzing an investor's financial risk tolerance.
- Describe the investment constraints of liquidity, time horizon, tax concerns, legal and regulatory factors, and unique circumstances and their implications for the choice of portfolio assets.
- Explain the definition and specification of asset classes in relation to asset allocation.
- Discuss the principles of portfolio construction and the role of asset allocation in relation to the IPS.

SUMMARY OVERVIEW

- The IPS is the starting point of the portfolio management process. Without a full understanding of the client's situation and requirements, it is unlikely that successful results will be achieved.
- The IPS can take a variety of forms. A typical format will include the client's investment objectives and also list the constraints that apply to the client's portfolio.
- The client's objectives are specified in terms of risk tolerance and return requirements.
- The constraints section covers factors that need to be considered when constructing a portfolio for the client that meets the objectives. The typical constraint categories are liquidity requirements, time horizon, regulatory requirements, tax status, and unique needs.
- Risk objectives are specifications for portfolio risk that reflect the risk tolerance of the client. Quantitative risk objectives can be absolute or relative or a combination of the two.

- The client's overall risk tolerance is a function of the client's ability to accept risk and their "risk attitude," which can be considered the client's willingness to take risk.
- The client's return objectives can be stated on an absolute or a relative basis. As an example of an absolute objective, the client may want to achieve a particular percentage rate of return. Alternatively, the return objective can be stated on a relative basis, for example, relative to a benchmark return.
- The liquidity section of the IPS should state what the client's requirements are to draw cash from the portfolio.
- The time horizon section of the IPS should state the time horizon over which the investor is investing. This horizon may be the period during which the portfolio is accumulating before any assets need to be withdrawn.
- Tax status varies among investors and a client's tax status should be stated in the IPS.
- The IPS should state any legal or regulatory restrictions that constrain the investment of the portfolio.
- The unique circumstances section of the IPS should cover any other aspect of a client's circumstances that is likely to have a material impact on the composition of the portfolio; for example, any religious or ethical preferences.
- Asset classes are the building blocks of an asset allocation. An asset class is a category of assets that have similar characteristics, attributes, and risk/return relationships. Traditionally, investors have distinguished cash, equities, bonds, and real estate as the major asset classes.
- A strategic asset allocation results from combining the constraints and objectives articulated in the IPS and capital market expectations regarding the asset classes.
- As time goes on, a client's asset allocation will drift from the target allocation, and the amount of allowable drift as well as a rebalancing policy should be formalized.
- In addition to taking systematic risk, an investment committee may choose to take tactical asset allocation risk or security selection risk. The amount of return attributable to these decisions can be measured.

PROBLEMS

1. Which of the following is *least* important as a reason for a written investment policy statement (IPS)?

   A. The IPS may be required by regulation.
   B. Having a written IPS is part of best practice for a portfolio manager.
   C. Having a written IPS ensures the client's risk and return objectives can be achieved.

2. Which of the following *best* describes the underlying rationale for a written investment policy statement (IPS)?

   A. A written IPS communicates a plan for trying to achieve investment success.
   B. A written IPS provides investment managers with a ready defense against client lawsuits.
   C. A written IPS allows investment managers to instruct clients about the proper use and purpose of investments.

3. A written investment policy statement (IPS) is *most* likely to succeed if:

   A. Created by a software program to assure consistent quality.
   B. It is a collaborative effort of the client and the portfolio manager.
   C. It reflects the investment philosophy of the portfolio manager.

4. The section of the investment policy statement (IPS) that provides information about how policy may be executed, including investment constraints, is *best* described as the:
   A. Investment Objectives.
   B. Investment Guidelines.
   C. Statement of Duties and Responsibilities.
5. Which of the following is *least* likely to be placed in the appendices to an investment policy statement (IPS)?
   A. Rebalancing Policy.
   B. Strategic Asset Allocation.
   C. Statement of Duties and Responsibilities.
6. Which of the following typical topics in an investment policy statement (IPS) is *most* closely linked to the client's "distinctive needs"?
   A. Procedures.
   B. Investment Guidelines.
   C. Statement of Duties and Responsibilities.
7. An investment policy statement that includes a return objective of outperforming the FTSE 100 by 120 basis points is *best* characterized as having a(n):
   A. Relative return objective.
   B. Absolute return objective.
   C. Arbitrage-based return objective.
8. Risk assessment questionnaires for investment management clients are *most* useful in measuring:
   A. Value at risk.
   B. Ability to take risk.
   C. Willingness to take risk.
9. Which of the following is *best* characterized as a relative risk objective?
   A. Value at risk for the fund will not exceed US$3 million.
   B. The fund will not underperform the DAX by more than 250 basis points.
   C. The fund will not lose more than €2.5 million in the coming 12-month period.
10. In preparing an investment policy statement, which of the following is *most* difficult to quantify?
    A. Time horizon.
    B. Ability to accept risk.
    C. Willingness to accept risk.
11. After interviewing a client in order to prepare a written investment policy statement (IPS), you have established the following:
    - The client has earnings that vary dramatically between £30,000 and £70,000 (pre-tax) depending on weather patterns in Britain.
    - In three of the previous five years, the after-tax income of the client has been less than £20,000.
    - The client's mother is dependent on her son (the client) for approximately £9,000 per year support.

- The client's own subsistence needs are approximately £12,000 per year.
- The client has more than 10 years experience trading investments including commodity futures, stock options, and selling stock short.
- The client's responses to a standard risk assessment questionnaire suggest he has above average risk tolerance.

The client is *best* described as having a:

A. Low ability to take risk, but a high willingness to take risk.
B. High ability to take risk, but a low willingness to take risk.
C. High ability to take risk and a high willingness to take risk.

12. After interviewing a client in order to prepare a written investment policy statement (IPS), you have established the following:

    - The client has earnings that have exceeded €120,000 (pre-tax) each year for the past five years.
    - She has no dependents.
    - The client's subsistence needs are approximately €45,000 per year.
    - The client states that she feels uncomfortable with her lack of understanding of securities markets.
    - All of the client's current savings are invested in short-term securities guaranteed by an agency of her national government.
    - The client's responses to a standard risk assessment questionnaire suggest she has low risk tolerance.

    The client is *best* described as having a:

    A. Low ability to take risk, but a high willingness to take risk.
    B. High ability to take risk, but a low willingness to take risk.
    C. High ability to take risk and a high willingness to take risk.

13. A client who is a 34-year old widow with two healthy young children (aged 5 and 7) has asked you to help her form an investment policy statement. She has been employed as an administrative assistant in a bureau of her national government for the previous 12 years. She has two primary financial goals—her retirement and providing for the college education of her children. This client's time horizon is *best* described as being:

    A. Long term.
    B. Short term.
    C. Medium term.

14. The timing of payouts for property and casualty insurers is unpredictable ("lumpy") in comparison with the timing of payouts for life insurance companies. Therefore, in general, property and casualty insurers have:

    A. Lower liquidity needs than life insurance companies.
    B. Greater liquidity needs than life insurance companies.
    C. A higher return objective than life insurance companies.

15. A client who is a director of a publicly listed corporation is required by law to refrain from trading that company's stock at certain points of the year when disclosure of financial results are pending. In preparing a written investment policy statement (IPS) for this client, this restriction on trading:

A. Is irrelevant to the IPS.
B. Should be included in the IPS.
C. Makes it illegal for the portfolio manager to work with this client.

16. Consider the pairwise correlations of monthly returns of the following asset classes:

	Brazilian Equities	East Asian Equities	European Equities	U.S. Equities
Brazilian equities	1.00	0.70	0.85	0.76
East Asian equities	0.70	1.00	0.91	0.88
European equities	0.85	0.91	1.00	0.90
U.S. equities	0.76	0.88	0.90	1.00

Based solely on the information in the above table, which equity asset class is *most* sharply distinguished from U.S. equities?

A. Brazilian equities.
B. European equities.
C. East Asian equities.

17. Returns on asset classes are *best* described as being a function of:

A. The failure of arbitrage.
B. Exposure to the idiosyncratic risks of those asset classes.
C. Exposure to sets of systematic factors relevant to those asset classes.

18. In defining asset classes as part of the strategic asset allocation decision, pairwise correlations within asset classes should generally be:

A. Equal to correlations among asset classes.
B. Lower than correlations among asset classes.
C. Higher than correlations among asset classes.

19. Tactical asset allocation is *best* described as:

A. Attempts to exploit arbitrage possibilities among asset classes.
B. The decision to deliberately deviate from the policy portfolio.
C. Selecting asset classes with the desired exposures to sources of systematic risk in an investment portfolio.

20. Investing the majority of the portfolio on a passive or low active risk basis while a minority of the assets is managed aggressively in smaller portfolios is *best* described as:

A. The core–satellite approach.
B. A top-down investment policy.
C. A delta-neutral hedge approach.

CHAPTER 8

OVERVIEW OF EQUITY SECURITIES

LEARNING OUTCOMES

After completing this chapter, you will be able to do the following:

- Discuss the importance and relative performance of equity securities in global financial markets.
- Discuss the characteristics of various types of equity securities.
- Distinguish between public and private equity securities.
- Discuss the differences in voting rights and other ownership characteristics among various equity classes.
- Discuss the methods for investing in nondomestic equity securities.
- Compare and contrast the risk and return characteristics of various types of equity securities.
- Explain the role of equity securities in the financing of a company's assets and creating company value.
- Distinguish between the market value and book value of equity securities.
- Compare and contrast a company's cost of equity, its (accounting) return on equity, and investors' required rates of return.

SUMMARY OVERVIEW

- Common shares represent an ownership interest in a company and give investors a claim on its operating performance, the opportunity to participate in the corporate decision-making process, and a claim on the company's net assets in the case of liquidation.
- Callable common shares give the issuer the right to buy back the shares from shareholders at a price determined when the shares are originally issued.
- Putable common shares give shareholders the right to sell the shares back to the issuer at a price specified when the shares are originally issued.
- Preference shares are a form of equity in which payments made to preference shareholders take precedence over any payments made to common stockholders.
- Cumulative preference shares are preference shares on which dividend payments are accrued so that any payments omitted by the company must be paid before another

dividend can be paid to common shareholders. Noncumulative preference shares have no such provisions, implying that the dividend payments are at the company's discretion and are thus similar to payments made to common shareholders.

- Participating preference shares allow investors to receive the standard preferred dividend plus the opportunity to receive a share of corporate profits above a prespecified amount. Nonparticipating preference shares allow investors to simply receive the initial investment plus any accrued dividends in the event of liquidation.
- Callable and putable preference shares provide issuers and investors with the same rights and obligations as their common share counterparts.
- Private equity securities are issued primarily to institutional investors in private placements and do not trade in secondary equity markets. There are three types of private equity investments: venture capital, leveraged buyouts, and private investments in public equity (PIPEs).
- The objective of private equity investing is to increase the ability of the company's management to focus on its operating activities for long-term value creation. The strategy is to take the "private" company "public" after certain profit and other benchmarks have been met.
- Depository receipts are securities that trade like ordinary shares on a local exchange but which represent an economic interest in a foreign company. They allow the publicly listed shares of foreign companies to be traded on an exchange outside their domestic market.
- American depository receipts are U.S. dollar-denominated securities trading much like standard U.S. securities on U.S. markets. Global depository receipts are similar to ADRs but contain certain restrictions in terms of their ability to be resold among investors.
- Underlying characteristics of equity securities can greatly affect their risk and return.
- A company's accounting return on equity is the total return that it earns on shareholders' book equity.
- A company's cost of equity is the minimum rate of return that stockholders require the company to pay them for investing in its equity.

PROBLEMS

1. Which of the following is *not* a characteristic of common equity?

   A. It represents an ownership interest in the company.
   B. Shareholders participate in the decision-making process.
   C. The company is obligated to make periodic dividend payments.

2. The type of equity voting right that grants one vote for each share of equity owned is referred to as:

   A. Proxy voting.
   B. Statutory voting.
   C. Cumulative voting.

3. All of the following are characteristics of preference shares *except*:

   A. They are either callable or putable.
   B. They generally do not have voting rights.
   C. They do not share in the operating performance of the company.

4. Participating preference shares entitle shareholders to:
   A. Participate in the decision-making process of the company.
   B. Convert their shares into a specified number of common shares.
   C. Receive an additional dividend if the company's profits exceed a predetermined level.

5. Which of the following statements about private equity securities is *incorrect*?
   A. They cannot be sold on secondary markets.
   B. They have market-determined quoted prices.
   C. They are primarily issued to institutional investors.

6. Venture capital investments:
   A. Can be publicly traded.
   B. Do not require a long-term commitment of funds.
   C. Provide mezzanine financing to early-stage companies.

7. Which of the following statements *most accurately* describes one difference between private and public equity firms?
   A. Private equity firms are focused more on short-term results than public firms.
   B. Private equity firms' regulatory and investor relations operations are less costly than those of public firms.
   C. Private equity firms are incentivized to be more open with investors about governance and compensation than public firms.

8. Emerging markets have benefited from recent trends in international markets. Which of the following has *not* been a benefit of these trends?
   A. Emerging market companies do not have to worry about a lack of liquidity in their home equity markets.
   B. Emerging market companies have found it easier to raise capital in the markets of developed countries.
   C. Emerging market companies have benefited from the stability of foreign exchange markets.

9. When investing in unsponsored depository receipts, the voting rights to the shares in the trust belong to:
   A. The depository bank.
   B. The investors in the depository receipts.
   C. The issuer of the shares held in the trust.

10. With respect to Level III sponsored ADRs, which of the following is *least likely* to be accurate? They:
    A. Have low listing fees.
    B. Are traded on the NYSE, NASDAQ, and AMEX.
    C. Are used to raise equity capital in U.S. markets.

11. A basket of listed depository receipts, or an exchange-traded fund, would *most likely* be used for:
    A. Gaining exposure to a single equity.
    B. Hedging exposure to a single equity.
    C. Gaining exposure to multiple equities.

12. Calculate the total return on a share of equity using the following data:
    Purchase price: $50
    Sale price: $42
    Dividend paid during holding period: $2

    A. −12.0%
    B. −14.3%
    C. −16.0%

13. If a U.S.-based investor purchases a euro-denominated ETF and the euro subsequently depreciates in value relative to the dollar, the investor will have a total return that is:

    A. Lower than the ETF's total return.
    B. Higher than the ETF's total return.
    C. The same as the ETF's total return.

14. Which of the following is *incorrect* about the risk of an equity security? The risk of an equity security is:

    A. Based on the uncertainty of its cash flows.
    B. Based on the uncertainty of its future price.
    C. Measured using the standard deviation of its dividends.

15. From an investor's point of view, which of the following equity securities is the *least* risky?

    A. Putable preference shares.
    B. Callable preference shares.
    C. Noncallable preference shares.

16. Which of the following is *least likely* to be a reason for a company to issue equity securities on the primary market?

    A. To raise capital.
    B. To increase liquidity.
    C. To increase return on equity.

17. Which of the following is *not* a primary goal of raising equity capital?

    A. To finance the purchase of long-lived assets.
    B. To finance the company's revenue-generating activities.
    C. To ensure that the company continues as a going concern.

18. Which of the following statements is *most accurate* in describing a company's book value?

    A. Book value increases when a company retains its net income.
    B. Book value is usually equal to the company's market value.
    C. The ultimate goal of management is to maximize book value.

19. Calculate the book value of a company using the following information:

Number of shares outstanding	100,000
Price per share	€52
Total assets	€12,000,000
Total liabilities	€7,500,000
Net Income	€2,000,000

A. €4,500,000
B. €5,200,000
C. €6,500,000

20. Which of the following statements is *least accurate* in describing a company's market value?

A. Management's decisions do not influence the company's market value.
B. Increases in book value may not be reflected in the company's market value.
C. Market value reflects the collective and differing expectations of investors.

21. Calculate the 2009 return on equity (ROE) of a stable company using the following data:

Total sales	£2,500,000
Net income	£2,000,000
Beginning of year total assets	£50,000,000
Beginning of year total liabilities	£35,000,000
Number of shares outstanding at the end of 2009	1,000,000
Price per share at the end of 2009	£20

A. 10.0%
B. 13.3%
C. 16.7%

22. Holding all other factors constant, which of the following situations will *most likely* lead to an increase in a company's return on equity?

A. The market price of the company's shares increases.
B. Net income increases at a slower rate than shareholders' equity.
C. The company issues debt to repurchase outstanding shares of equity.

23. Which of the following measures is the *most difficult* to estimate?

A. The cost of debt.
B. The cost of equity.
C. Investors' required rate of return on debt.

24. A company's cost of equity is often used as a proxy for investors':

A. Average required rate of return.
B. Minimum required rate of return.
C. Maximum required rate of return.

CHAPTER 9

INTRODUCTION TO INDUSTRY AND COMPANY ANALYSIS

LEARNING OUTCOMES

After completing this chapter, you will be able to do the following:

- Explain the uses of industry analysis and the relation of industry analysis to company analysis.
- Compare and contrast the methods by which companies can be grouped, current industry classification systems, and classify a company, given a description of its activities and the classification system.
- Explain the factors that affect the sensitivity of a company to the business cycle and the uses and limitations of industry and company descriptors such as "growth," "defensive," and "cyclical."
- Explain the relation of "peer group," as used in equity valuation, to a company's industry classification.
- Discuss the elements that need to be covered in a thorough industry analysis.
- Illustrate demographic, governmental, social, and technological influences on industry growth, profitability, and risk.
- Describe product and industry life-cycle models, classify an industry as to life-cycle phase (e.g., embryonic, growth, shakeout, maturity, or decline) based on a description of it, and discuss the limitations of the life-cycle concept in forecasting industry performance.
- Explain the effects of industry concentration, ease of entry, and capacity on return on invested capital and pricing power.
- Discuss the principles of strategic analysis of an industry.
- Compare and contrast the characteristics of representative industries from the various economic sectors.
- Describe the elements that should be covered in a thorough company analysis.

SUMMARY OVERVIEW

- Company analysis and industry analysis are closely interrelated. Company and industry analysis together can provide insight into sources of industry revenue growth and competitors' market shares and thus the future of an individual company's top-line growth and bottom-line profitability.

- Industry analysis is useful for
  - Understanding a company's business and business environment.
  - Identifying active equity investment opportunities.
  - Formulating an industry or sector rotation strategy.
  - Portfolio performance attribution.
- The three main approaches to classifying companies are
  - Products and/or services supplied.
  - Business-cycle sensitivities.
  - Statistical similarities.
- Commercial industry classification systems include
  - Global Industry Classification Standard.
  - Russell Global Sectors.
  - Industry Classification Benchmark.
- Governmental industry classification systems include
  - International Standard Industrial Classification of All Economic Activities.
  - Statistical Classification of Economic Activities in the European Community.
  - Australian and New Zealand Standard Industrial Classification.
  - North American Industry Classification System.
- A limitation of current classification systems is that the narrowest classification unit assigned to a company generally cannot be assumed to constitute its peer group for the purposes of detailed fundamental comparisons or valuation.
- A peer group is a group of companies engaged in similar business activities whose economics and valuation are influenced by closely related factors.
- Steps in constructing a preliminary list of peer companies:
  - Examine commercial classification systems if available. These systems often provide a useful starting point for identifying companies operating in the same industry.
  - Review the subject company's annual report for a discussion of the competitive environment. Companies frequently cite specific competitors.
  - Review competitors' annual reports to identify other potential comparables.
  - Review industry trade publications to identify additional peer companies.
  - Confirm that each comparable or peer company derives a significant portion of its revenue and operating profit from a similar business activity as the subject company.
- Not all industries are created equal. Some are highly competitive, with many companies struggling to earn returns in excess of their cost of capital, and other industries have attractive characteristics that enable a majority of industry participants to generate healthy profits.
- Differing competitive environments are determined by the structural attributes of the industry. For this important reason, industry analysis is a vital complement to company analysis. The analyst needs to understand the context in which a company operates to fully understand the opportunities and threats that a company faces.
- The framework for strategic analysis known as "Porter's five forces" can provide a useful starting point. Porter maintains that the profitability of companies in an industry is determined by five forces: (1) The influence or threat of new entrants, which in turn is determined

by economies of scale, brand loyalty, absolute cost advantages, customer switching costs, and government regulation; (2) the influence or threat of substitute products; (3) the bargaining power of customers, which is a function of switching costs among customers and the ability of customers to produce their own product; (4) the bargaining power of suppliers, which is a function of the feasibility of product substitution, the concentration of the buyer and supplier groups, and switching costs and entry costs in each case; and (5) the intensity of rivalry among established companies, which in turn is a function of industry competitive structure, demand conditions, cost conditions, and the height of exit barriers.

- The concept of barriers to entry refers to the ease with which new competitors can challenge incumbents and can be an important factor in determining the competitive environment of an industry. If new competitors can easily enter the industry, the industry is likely to be highly competitive because incumbents that attempt to raise prices will be undercut by newcomers. As a result, industries with low barriers to entry tend to have low pricing power. Conversely, if incumbents are protected by barriers to entry, they may enjoy a more benign competitive environment that gives them greater pricing power over their customers because they do not have to worry about being undercut by upstarts.
- Industry concentration is often, although not always, a sign that an industry may have pricing power and rational competition. Industry fragmentation is a much stronger signal, however, that the industry is competitive and pricing power is limited.
- The effect of industry capacity on pricing is clear: Tight capacity gives participants more pricing power because demand for products or services exceeds supply; overcapacity leads to price-cutting and a highly competitive environment as excess supply chases demand. The analyst should think about not only current capacity conditions but also future changes in capacity levels—how long it takes for supply and demand to come into balance and what effect that process has on industry pricing power and returns.
- Examining the market share stability of an industry over time is similar to thinking about barriers to entry and the frequency with which new players enter an industry. Stable market shares typically indicate less competitive industries, whereas unstable market shares often indicate highly competitive industries with limited pricing power.
- An industry's position in its life cycle often has a large impact on its competitive dynamics, so it is important to keep this positioning in mind when performing strategic analysis of an industry. Industries, like individual companies, tend to evolve over time and usually experience significant changes in the rate of growth and levels of profitability along the way. Just as an investment in an individual company requires careful monitoring, industry analysis is a continuous process that must be repeated over time to identify changes that may be occurring.
- A useful framework for analyzing the evolution of an industry is an industry life-cycle model, which identifies the sequential stages that an industry typically goes through. The five stages of an industry life cycle according to the Hill and Jones model are
  - Embryonic.
  - Growth.
  - Shakeout.
  - Mature.
  - Decline.
- Price competition and thinking like a customer are important factors that are often overlooked when analyzing an industry. Whatever factors most influence customer

purchasing decisions are also likely to be the focus of competitive rivalry in the industry. Broadly, industries for which price is a large factor in customer purchase decisions tend to be more competitive than industries in which customers value other attributes more highly.
- External influences on industry growth, profitability, and risk include
  - Technology.
  - Demographics.
  - Government.
  - Social factors.
- Company analysis takes place after the analyst has gained an understanding of the company's external environment and includes answering questions about how the company will respond to the threats and opportunities presented by the external environment. This intended response is the individual company's competitive strategy. The analyst should seek to determine whether the strategy is primarily defensive or offensive in its nature and how the company intends to implement it.
- Porter identifies two chief competitive strategies:
  - A low-cost strategy (cost leadership) is one in which companies strive to become the low-cost producers and to gain market share by offering their products and services at lower prices than their competition while still making a profit margin sufficient to generate a superior rate of return based on the higher revenues achieved.
  - A product/service differentiation strategy is one in which companies attempt to establish themselves as the suppliers or producers of products and services that are unique either in quality, type, or means of distribution. To be successful, the companies' price premiums must be above their costs of differentiation and the differentiation must be appealing to customers and sustainable over time.
- A checklist for company analysis includes a thorough investigation of
  - Corporate profile.
  - Industry characteristics.
  - Demand for products/services.
  - Supply of products/services.
  - Pricing.
  - Financial ratios.
- Spreadsheet modeling of financial statements to analyze and forecast revenues, operating and net income, and cash flows has become one of the most widely used tools in company analysis. Spreadsheet modeling can be used to quantify the effects of the changes in certain swing factors on the various financial statements. The analyst should be aware that the output of the model will depend significantly on the assumptions that are made.

PROBLEMS

1. Which of the following is *least likely* to involve industry analysis?

   A. Sector rotation strategy.
   B. Top-down fundamental investing.
   C. Tactical asset allocation strategy.

2. A sector rotation strategy involves investing in a sector by:
   A. Making regular investments in it.
   B. Investing in a pre-selected group of sectors on a rotating basis.
   C. Timing investment to take advantage of business-cycle conditions.
3. Which of the following information about a company would *most likely* depend on an industry analysis? The company's:
   A. Dividend policy.
   B. Competitive environment.
   C. Trends in corporate expenses.
4. Which industry classification system uses a three-tier classification system?
   A. Russell Global Sectors.
   B. Industry Classification Benchmark.
   C. Global Industry Classification Standard.
5. In which sector would a manufacturer of personal care products be classified?
   A. Health care.
   B. Consumer staples.
   C. Consumer discretionary.
6. Which of the following statements about commercial and government industry classification systems is *most* accurate?
   A. Many commercial classification systems include private for-profit companies.
   B. Both commercial and government classification systems exclude not-for-profit companies.
   C. Commercial classification systems are generally updated more frequently than government classification systems.
7. Which of the following is *not* a limitation of the cyclical/noncyclical descriptive approach to classifying companies?
   A. A cyclical company may have a growth component in it.
   B. Business-cycle sensitivity is a discrete phenomenon rather than a continuous spectrum.
   C. A global company can experience economic expansion in one part of the world while experiencing recession in another part.
8. A company that is sensitive to the business cycle would *most likely*:
   A. Not have growth opportunities.
   B. Experience below-average fluctuation in demand.
   C. Sell products that the customer can purchase at a later date if necessary.
9. Which of the following factors would *most likely* be a limitation of applying business-cycle analysis to global industry analysis?
   A. Some industries are relatively insensitive to the business cycle.
   B. Correlations of security returns between different world markets are relatively low.
   C. One region or country of the world may experience recession while another region experiences expansion.

10. Which of the following statements about peer groups is *most* accurate?
    A. Constructing a peer group for a company follows a standardized process.
    B. Commercial industry classification systems often provide a starting point for constructing a peer group.
    C. A peer group is generally composed of all the companies in the most narrowly defined category used by the commercial industry classification system.

11. With regard to forming a company's peer group, which of the following statements is *not* correct?
    A. Comments from the management of the company about competitors are generally not used when selecting the peer group.
    B. The higher the proportion of revenue and operating profit of the peer company derived from business activities similar to the subject company, the more meaningful the comparison.
    C. Comparing the company's performance measures with those for a potential peer-group company is of limited value when the companies are exposed to different stages of the business cycle.

12. When selecting companies for inclusion in a peer group, a company operating in three different business segments would:
    A. Be in only one peer group.
    B. Possibly be in more than one peer group.
    C. Not be included in any peer group.

13. An industry that *most likely* has both high barriers to entry and high barriers to exit is the:
    A. Restaurant industry.
    B. Advertising industry.
    C. Automobile industry.

14. Which factor is *most likely* associated with stable market share?
    A. Low switching costs.
    B. Low barriers to entry.
    C. Slow pace of product innovation.

15. Which of the following companies *most likely* has the greatest ability to quickly increase its capacity?
    A. Restaurant.
    B. Steel producer.
    C. Legal services provider.

16. A population that is rapidly aging would *most likely* cause the growth rate of the industry producing eyeglasses and contact lenses to:
    A. Decrease.
    B. Increase.
    C. Not change.

17. If over a long period of time a country's average level of educational accomplishment increases, this development would *most likely* lead to the country's amount of income spent on consumer discretionary goods to:

A. Decrease.
B. Increase.
C. Not change.

18. If the technology for an industry involves high fixed capital investment, then one way to seek higher profit growth is by pursuing:

    A. Economies of scale.
    B. Diseconomies of scale.
    C. Removal of features that differentiate the product or service provided.

19. Which of the following life-cycle phases is typically characterized by high prices?

    A. Mature.
    B. Growth.
    C. Embryonic.

20. In which of the following life-cycle phases are price wars *most likely* to be absent?

    A. Mature.
    B. Decline.
    C. Growth.

21. When graphically depicting the life-cycle model for an industry as a curve, the variables on the axes are:

    A. Price and time.
    B. Demand and time.
    C. Demand and stage of the life cycle.

22. Which of the following is *most likely* a characteristic of a concentrated industry?

    A. Infrequent, tacit coordination.
    B. Difficulty in monitoring other industry members.
    C. Industry members attempting to avoid competition on price.

23. Which of the following industry characteristics is generally *least likely* to produce high returns on capital?

    A. High barriers to entry.
    B. High degree of concentration.
    C. Short lead time to build new plants.

24. An industry with high barriers to entry and weak pricing power *most likely* has:

    A. High barriers to exit.
    B. Stable market shares.
    C. Significant numbers of issued patents.

25. Economic value is created for an industry's shareholders when the industry earns a return:

    A. Below the cost of capital.
    B. Equal to the cost of capital.
    C. Above the cost of capital.

26. Which of the following is *not* one of Porter's five forces?
    A. Intensity of rivalry.
    B. Bargaining power of suppliers.
    C. Threat of government intervention.
27. Which of the following industries is *most likely* to be characterized as concentrated with strong pricing power?
    A. Asset management.
    B. Alcoholic beverages.
    C. Household and personal products.
28. Which of the following industries is *most likely* to be considered to have the lowest barriers to entry?
    A. Oil services.
    B. Confections and candy.
    C. Branded pharmaceuticals.
29. With respect to competitive strategy, a company with a successful cost leadership strategy is *most likely* characterized by:
    A. A low cost of capital.
    B. Reduced market share.
    C. The ability to offer products at higher prices than competitors.
30. When conducting a company analysis, the analysis of demand for a company's product is *least likely* to consider the:
    A. Company's cost structure.
    B. Motivations of the customer base.
    C. Product's differentiating characteristics.
31. Which of the following statements about company analysis is *most* accurate?
    A. The complexity of spreadsheet modeling ensures precise forecasts of financial statements.
    B. The interpretation of financial ratios should focus on comparing the company's results over time but not with competitors.
    C. The corporate profile would include a description of the company's business, investment activities, governance, and strengths and weaknesses.

CHAPTER 10

EQUITY VALUATION: CONCEPTS AND BASIC TOOLS

LEARNING OUTCOMES

After completing this chapter, you will be able to do the following:

- Evaluate whether a security, given its current market price and a value estimate, is overvalued, fairly valued, or undervalued by the market.
- Describe major categories of equity valuation models.
- Explain the rationale for using present-value of cash flow models to value equity and describe the dividend discount and free cash flow to equity models.
- Calculate the intrinsic value of a noncallable, nonconvertible preferred stock.
- Calculate and interpret the intrinsic value of an equity security based on the Gordon (constant) growth dividend discount model or a two-stage dividend discount model, as appropriate.
- Identify companies for which the constant growth or a multistage dividend discount model is appropriate.
- Explain the rationale for using price multiples to value equity and distinguish between multiples based on comparables versus multiples based on fundamentals.
- Calculate and interpret the following multiples: price to earnings, price to an estimate of operating cash flow, price to sales, and price to book value.
- Explain the use of enterprise value multiples in equity valuation and demonstrate the use of enterprise value multiples to estimate equity value.
- Explain asset-based valuation models and demonstrate the use of asset-based models to calculate equity value.
- Explain the advantages and disadvantages of each category of valuation model.

SUMMARY OVERVIEW

- An analyst estimating intrinsic value is implicitly questioning the market's estimate of value.
- If the estimated value exceeds the market price, the analyst infers the security is *undervalued*. If the estimated value equals the market price, the analyst infers the security is *fairly*

valued. If the estimated value is less than the market price, the analyst infers the security is *overvalued*. Because of the uncertainties involved in valuation, an analyst may require that value estimates differ markedly from market price before concluding that a misvaluation exists.

- Analysts often use more than one valuation model because of concerns about the applicability of any particular model and the variability in estimates that result from changes in inputs.
- Three major categories of equity valuation models are present value, multiplier, and asset-based valuation models.
- Present value models estimate value as the present value of expected future benefits.
- Multiplier models estimate intrinsic value based on a multiple of some fundamental variable.
- Asset-based valuation models estimate value based on the estimated value of assets and liabilities.
- The choice of model will depend upon the availability of information to input into the model and the analyst's confidence in both the information and the appropriateness of the model.
- In the dividend discount model, value is estimated as the present value of expected future dividends.
- In the free cash flow to equity model, value is estimated as the present value of expected future free cash flow to equity.
- The Gordon growth model, a simple DDM, estimates value as $D_1/(r-g)$.
- The two-stage dividend discount model estimates value as the sum of the present values of dividends over a short-term period of high growth and the present value of the terminal value at the end of the period of high growth. The terminal value is estimated using the Gordon growth model.
- The choice of dividend model is based upon the patterns assumed with respect to future dividends.
- Multiplier models typically use multiples of the form: P/measure of fundamental variable or EV/measure of fundamental variable.
- Multiples can be based upon fundamentals or comparables.
- Asset-based valuations models estimate value of equity as the value of the assets less the value of liabilities.

PROBLEMS

1. An analyst estimates the intrinsic value of a stock to be in the range of €17.85 to €21.45. The current market price of the stock is €24.35. This stock is *most likely*:

   A. Overvalued.
   B. Undervalued.
   C. Fairly valued.

2. An analyst determines the intrinsic value of an equity security to be equal to $55. If the current price is $47, the equity is *most likely*:

   A. Undervalued.
   B. Fairly valued.
   C. Overvalued.

3. In asset-based valuation models, the intrinsic value of a common share of stock is based on the:

   A. Estimated market value of the company's assets.
   B. Estimated market value of the company's assets plus liabilities.
   C. Estimated market value of the company's assets minus liabilities.

4. Which of the following is *most likely* used in a present value model?

   A. Enterprise value.
   B. Price to free cash flow.
   C. Free cash flow to equity.

5. Book value is *least likely* to be considered when using:

   A. A multiplier model.
   B. An asset-based valuation model.
   C. A present value model.

6. An analyst is attempting to calculate the intrinsic value of a company and has gathered the following company data: EBITDA, total market value, and market value of cash and short-term investments, liabilities, and preferred shares. The analyst is *least likely* to use:

   A. A multiplier model.
   B. A discounted cash flow model.
   C. An asset-based valuation model.

7. An analyst who bases the calculation of intrinsic value on dividend-paying capacity rather than expected dividends will *most likely* use the:

   A. Dividend discount model.
   B. Free cash flow to equity model.
   C. Cash flow from operations model.

8. An investor expects to purchase shares of common stock today and sell them after two years. The investor has estimated dividends for the next two years, D_1 and D_2, and the selling price of the stock two years from now, P_2. According to the dividend discount model, the intrinsic value of the stock today is the present value of:

   A. Next year's dividend, D_1.
   B. Future expected dividends, D_1 and D_2.
   C. Future expected dividends and price—D_1, D_2 and P_2.

9. In the free cash flow to equity (FCFE) model, the intrinsic value of a share of stock is calculated as:

   A. The present value of future expected FCFE.
   B. The present value of future expected FCFE plus net borrowing.
   C. The present value of future expected FCFE minus fixed capital investment.

10. With respect to present value models, which of the following statements is *most accurate*?

   A. Present value models can be used only if a stock pays a dividend.
   B. Present value models can be used only if a stock pays a dividend or is expected to pay a dividend.
   C. Present value models can be used for stocks that currently pay a dividend, are expected to pay a dividend, or are not expected to pay a dividend.

11. A Canadian life insurance company has an issue of 4.80 percent, $25 par value, perpetual, nonconvertible, noncallable preferred shares outstanding. The required rate of return on similar issues is 4.49 percent. The intrinsic value of a preferred share is *closest to*:

    A. $25.00.
    B. $26.75.
    C. $28.50.

12. Two analysts estimating the value of a nonconvertible, noncallable, perpetual preferred stock with a constant dividend arrive at different estimated values. The *most likely* reason for the difference is that the analysts used different:

    A. Time horizons.
    B. Required rates of return.
    C. Estimated dividend growth rates.

13. The Beasley Corporation has just paid a dividend of $1.75 per share. If the required rate of return is 12.3 percent per year and dividends are expected to grow indefinitely at a constant rate of 9.2 percent per year, the intrinsic value of Beasley Corporation stock is *closest* to:

    A. $15.54.
    B. $56.45.
    C. $61.65.

14. An investor is considering the purchase of a common stock with a $2.00 annual dividend. The dividend is expected to grow at a rate of 4 percent annually. If the investor's required rate of return is 7 percent, the intrinsic value of the stock is *closest* to:

    A. $50.00.
    B. $66.67.
    C. $69.33.

15. An analyst gathers or estimates the following information about a stock:

Current price per share	€22.56
Current annual dividend per share	€1.60
Annual dividend growth rate for Years 1–4	9.00%
Annual dividend growth rate for Years 5+	4.00%
Required rate of return	12%

    Based on a dividend discount model, the stock is *most likely*:

    A. Undervalued.
    B. Fairly valued.
    C. Overvalued.

16. An analyst is attempting to value shares of the Dominion Company. The company has just paid a dividend of $0.58 per share. Dividends are expected to grow by 20 percent next year and 15 percent the year after that. From the third year onward, dividends are expected to grow at 5.6 percent per year indefinitely. If the required rate of return is 8.3 percent, the intrinsic value of the stock is *closest* to:

A. \$26.00.
B. \$27.00.
C. \$28.00.

17. Hideki Corporation has just paid a dividend of ¥450 per share. Annual dividends are expected to grow at the rate of 4 percent per year over the next four years. At the end of four years, shares of Hideki Corporation are expected to sell for ¥9000. If the required rate of return is 12 percent, the intrinsic value of a share of Hideki Corporation is *closest* to:

    A. ¥5,850.
    B. ¥7,220.
    C. ¥7,670.

18. The Gordon growth model can be used to value dividend-paying companies that are:

    A. Expected to grow very fast.
    B. In a mature phase of growth.
    C. Very sensitive to the business cycle.

19. The best model to use when valuing a young dividend-paying company that is just entering the growth phase is *most likely* the:

    A. Gordon growth model.
    B. Two-stage dividend discount model.
    C. Three-stage dividend discount model.

20. An equity analyst has been asked to estimate the intrinsic value of the common stock of Omega Corporation, a leading manufacturer of automobile seats. Omega is in a mature industry, and both its earnings and dividends are expected to grow at a rate of 3 percent annually. Which of the following is *most likely* to be the best model for determining the intrinsic value of an Omega share?

    A. Gordon growth model.
    B. Free cash flow to equity model.
    C. Multistage dividend discount model.

21. A price earnings ratio that is derived from the Gordon growth model is inversely related to the:

    A. Growth rate.
    B. Dividend payout ratio.
    C. Required rate of return.

22. The primary difference between P/E multiples based on comparables and P/E multiples based on fundamentals is that fundamentals-based P/Es take into account:

    A. Future expectations.
    B. The law of one price.
    C. Historical information.

23. An analyst makes the following statement: "Use of P/E and other multiples for analysis is not effective because the multiples are based on historical data and because not all companies have positive accounting earnings." The analyst's statement is *most likely*:

    A. Inaccurate with respect to both historical data and earnings.
    B. Accurate with respect to historical data and inaccurate with respect to earnings.
    C. Inaccurate with respect to historical data and accurate with respect to earnings.

24. An analyst has prepared a table of the average trailing 12-month price-to-earning (P/E), price-to-cash flow (P/CF), and price-to-sales (P/S) for the Tanaka Corporation for the years 2005 to 2008.

Year	P/E	P/CF	P/S
2005	4.9	5.4	1.2
2006	6.1	8.6	1.5
2007	8.3	7.3	1.9
2008	9.2	7.9	2.3

As of the date of the valuation in 2009, the trailing 12-month P/E, P/CF, and P/S are, respectively, 9.2, 8.0, and 2.5. Based on the information provided, the analyst may reasonably conclude that Tanaka shares are *most likely*:

A. Overvalued.
B. Undervalued.
C. Fairly valued.

25. An analyst has gathered the following information for the Oudin Corporation:
Expected earnings per share = €5.70
Expected dividends per share = €2.70
Dividends are expected to grow at 2.75 percent per year indefinitely
The required rate of return is 8.35 percent
Based on the information provided, the price/earnings multiple for Oudin is *closest* to:

A. 5.7.
B. 8.5.
C. 9.4.

26. An analyst gathers the following information about two companies:

	Alpha Corp.	Delta Co.
Current price per share	$57.32	$18.93
Last year's EPS	$3.82	$ 1.35
Current year's estimated EPS	$4.75	$ 1.40

Which of the following statements is *most accurate*?

A. Delta has the higher trailing P/E multiple and lower current estimated P/E multiple.
B. Alpha has the higher trailing P/E multiple and lower current estimated P/E multiple.
C. Alpha has the higher trailing P/E multiple and higher current estimated P/E multiple.

27. An analyst gathers the following information about similar companies in the banking sector:

	First Bank	Prime Bank	Pioneer Trust
P/B	1.10	0.60	0.60
P/E	8.40	11.10	8.30

Which of the companies is *most likely* to be undervalued?

A. First Bank.
B. Prime Bank.
C. Pioneer Trust.

28. The market value of equity for a company can be calculated as enterprise value:

A. Minus market value of debt, preferred stock, and short-term investments.
B. Plus market value of debt and preferred stock minus short-term investments.
C. Minus market value of debt and preferred stock plus short-term investments.

29. Which of the following statements regarding the calculation of the enterprise value multiple is *most likely* correct?

A. Operating income may be used instead of EBITDA.
B. EBITDA may not be used if company earnings are negative.
C. Book value of debt may be used instead of market value of debt.

30. An analyst has determined that the appropriate EV/EBITDA for Rainbow Company is 10.2. The analyst has also collected the following forecasted information for Rainbow Company:
EBITDA = $22,000,000
Market value of debt = $56,000,000
Cash = $1,500,000
The value of equity for Rainbow Company is *closest* to:

A. $169 million.
B. $224 million.
C. $281 million.

31. Enterprise value is most often determined as market capitalization of common equity and preferred stock minus the value of cash equivalents plus the:

A. Book value of debt.
B. Market value of debt.
C. Market value of long-term debt.

32. Asset-based valuation models are best suited to companies where the capital structure does not have a high proportion of:

A. Debt.
B. Intangible assets.
C. Current assets and liabilities.

33. Which of the following is *most likely* a reason for using asset-based valuation?

A. The analyst is valuing a privately held company.
B. The company has a relatively high level of intangible assets.
C. The market values of assets and liabilities are different from the balance sheet values.

34. A disadvantage of the EV method for valuing equity is that the following information may be difficult to obtain:

A. Operating income.
B. Market value of debt.
C. Market value of equity.

35. Which type of equity valuation model is *most likely* to be preferable when one is comparing similar companies?

    A. A multiplier model.
    B. A present value model.
    C. An asset based valuation model.

36. Which of the following is *most likely* considered a weakness of present value models?

    A. Present value models cannot be used for companies that do not pay dividends.
    B. Small changes in model assumptions and inputs can result in large changes in the computed intrinsic value of the security.
    C. The value of the security depends on the investor's holding period; thus, comparing valuations of different companies for different investors is difficult.

CHAPTER 11

EQUITY MARKET VALUATION

LEARNING OUTCOMES

After completing this chapter, you will be able to do the following:

- Explain the terms of the Cobb-Douglas production function and demonstrate how the function can be used to model growth in real output under the assumption of constant returns to scale.
- Evaluate the relative importance of growth in total factor productivity, in capital stock, and in labor input given relevant historical data.
- Demonstrate the use of the Cobb-Douglas production function in obtaining a discounted dividend model estimate of the intrinsic value of an equity market.
- Evaluate the sensitivity of equity market value estimates to changes in assumptions.
- Contrast top-down and bottom-up forecasts of the earnings per share of an equity market index.
- Explain and critique models of relative equity market valuation based on earnings and assets.
- Judge whether an equity market is under-, fairly, or overvalued based on a relative equity valuation model.

SUMMARY OVERVIEW

- The growth accounting equation allows one to decompose real GDP growth, $\Delta Y/Y$, into components that can be attributed to the observable factors: the growth of the capital stock, $\Delta K/K$, the output elasticity of capital, α, the growth in the labor force, $\Delta L/L$, the output elasticity of labor, $1 - \alpha$, and a residual factor—often called the Solow residual—that is the portion of growth left unaccounted for by increases in the standard factors of production, $\Delta A/A$.

$$\frac{\Delta Y}{Y} \approx \frac{\Delta A}{A} + \alpha\frac{\Delta K}{K} + (1-\alpha)\frac{\Delta L}{L}$$

- The existence of TFP growth, $\Delta A/A$, means that total output can grow at a faster rate than would be predicted simply from growth in accumulated capital stock and the labor force.

TFP is typically linked to innovation and technical progress. However, changes in work organization, government regulation, and the literacy and skills of the work force, as well as many other factors, also affect TFP.

- The inputs for the H-model include the initial growth rate, g_S, a period of years, N, where the dividend growth rate declines in a linear fashion, and a long-term dividend growth rate, g_L, that is expected to prevail to perpetuity beginning at the end of period N. With an initial annualized dividend rate D_0 and a discount rate to perpetuity of r, the formula for intrinsic value, V_0 according to the H-model is:

$$V_0 = \frac{D_0}{r - g_L}\left[(1+g_L) + \frac{N}{2}(g_S - g_L)\right]$$

- In top-down forecasting, analysts use macroeconomic forecasts to develop market forecasts and then make industry and security forecasts consistent with the market forecasts. In bottom-up forecasting, individual company forecasts are aggregated to industry forecasts, which in turn are aggregated to produce a market forecast.
- Bottom-up forecasts tend to be more optimistic than top-down forecasts. Top-down models can be slow in detecting cyclical turns if the current statistical relationships between economic variables deviate significantly from their historic norms.
- The Fed model is a theory of equity valuation that hypothesizes that the yield on long-term U.S. Treasury securities (usually defined as the 10-year T-note yield) should be equal to the S&P 500 earnings yield (usually defined as forward operating earnings divided by the index level) in equilibrium.
- A common criticism of the Fed model equilibrium is that it fails to incorporate the equity risk premium. The earnings yield can also be a poor measure of the true value of equities if significant growth opportunities exist. Some authors have also argued that the Fed model comparison is flawed because the earnings yield is real while the Treasury yield is nominal.
- The Yardeni model addresses some of the criticisms of the Fed model. As inputs, Yardeni used the Moody's A-rated corporate bond yield, y_B, the consensus five-year earnings growth forecast for the S&P 500 from Thomson Financial, LTEG, and the coefficient d, which represents a weighting factor measuring the importance the market assigns to the earnings projections. Yardeni found that the historical values for d averaged about 0.10. The formula for the Yardeni model is:

$$\frac{E_1}{P_0} = y_B - d \times \text{LTEG}$$

- Limitations of the Yardeni model include that the risk premium captured by the model is largely a default risk premium and not the future equity risk premium, which is unobservable. Also, the consensus five-year earnings growth forecast for the S&P 500 from Thomson Financial may not be sustainable and evidence suggests that the weighting factor varies significantly over time.
- Campbell and Shiller's P/10-year MA(E) has become a popular measure of market valuation. The numerator of P/10-year MA(E) is the real S&P 500 and the denominator is the moving average of the preceding 10 years of real reported earnings. "Real" denotes that the stock index and earnings are adjusted for inflation using the Consumer Price Index (CPI). The purpose of the 10-year moving average of real reported earnings is to control for business cycle effects on earnings and is based on recommendations from the seminal work of Graham and Dodd.

- Tobin's q is calculated at the individual company level as the market value of a company divided by the replacement cost of its assets. Smithers and Wright created an equity q that is the ratio of a company's market capitalization divided by net worth measured at replacement cost. Market-level measures may be computed for Tobin's q and equity q by a process of aggregation; these market-level measures may be used to form a valuation judgment about an equity market. Assuming that Tobin's q will revert to the comparison value, a Tobin's q below, at, or above the comparison value is interpreted as the market being under-, fairly, or overvalued. Strong economic arguments exist that both Tobin's q and equity q should be mean-reverting series.
- In practice, estimating replacement cost can be problematic due to the lack of liquid markets for many assets. Moreover, such items as human capital, trade secrets, copyrights and patents, and brand equity are intangible assets that are difficult to value.

PROBLEMS

1. Elizabeth Villeneuve is a senior economist at Proplus Financial Economics Consulting (Proplus). She is responsible for the valuation of equity markets in developing countries and is reviewing the preliminary report on Emerge Country prepared by one of her analysts, Danielle DeLaroche. Emerge Country is now experiencing stronger economic growth than most developed countries.

   DeLaroche has summarized in Exhibit A some of the assumptions contained in the report. In modeling the growth in the country's real output, she has used the Cobb-Douglas production function under the assumption of constant returns to scale and, in valuing the equity market, she has used the standard Gordon growth model with constant dividend growth rate.

   EXHIBIT A Assumptions for the Equity Index of Emerge Country

Annual dividend per share in 2008	450 CU*
Forecasted earnings per share in 2009	750 CU*
Forecasted annual growth in TFP	1.5%
Expected real growth rate of dividends to perpetuity	5.5%
Required real discount rate to perpetuity	7.5%

   *CU = currency unit of Emerge Country

   A. Based on the information in Exhibit A, calculate the equity index price level of Emerge Country implied by the Gordon growth model, as of 31 December 2008. Villeneuve is familiar with the Gordon growth model but not the H-model.
   B. Identify *two* variables that are needed in the H-model and not needed in the Gordon growth model.

   As an illustration of a relative value approach that can be used to support tactical asset allocation, DeLaroche has estimated that the forward operating earnings yield of the equity index in Emerge Country is 6 percent and that the medium-term government bond yield is 7 percent. She then applies the Fed model to the situation in Emerge Country.

   C. Based on the Fed model, determine whether the equity market is undervalued or overvalued and identify three criticisms of the Fed model.

Because most of Proplus's clients use strategies that require fundamental security analysis, Proplus uses both top-down and bottom-up approaches in all reports dealing with equity return forecasts.

D. Contrast the two forecasting approaches used by DeLaroche as they relate to industry analysis.

2. Don Murray, an economist, is president of the investment committee of a large U.S. pension plan. He is reviewing the plan's recent investment returns and finds that non-U.S. equity returns have been much higher than U.S. equity returns. Before making any changes to the plan's asset allocation, he has asked to meet with Susan McLean, CFA, who is responsible for the equity portion of the pension plan assets. Murray wants to discuss with McLean the current valuation levels of various equity markets.

Murray develops his own growth projections for the United States and for a hypothetical country (Hyp Country) that enjoys a well-developed economy but whose population is aging. These projections are shown in Exhibit B. In addition, Murray projects that output elasticity of capital equals 0.3 and 0.5 for the United States and Hyp Country, respectively.

EXHIBIT B Growth Projections (2010–2029)

Country	Growth in Total Factor Productivity	Growth in Capital Stock	Growth in Labor Input
United States	0.6%	3.5%	0.4%
Hyp Country	1.0%	3.3%	0.1%

A. Based on the information in Exhibit B, calculate the projected GDP growth for the United States for the period 2010–2029. Use the Cobb-Douglas production function and assume constant returns to scale.

Murray identifies two possible measures that the government of Hyp Country could implement and he wants to know how these measures would affect projected GDP growth for Hyp Country.

Measure 1: Lower the retirement age from 65 to 63, gradually over the next four-year period

Measure 2: Reduce subsidies to higher education over the next five years

B. For each of the growth measures identified by Murray in Exhibit B, indicate which growth factor is *most* affected. Justify your answers.

Murray is surprised that the bottom-up forecasts produced by McLean for the United States in the last five years have been consistently more optimistic than her top-down forecasts. As a result, he expresses doubt about the validity of either approach.

C. State *one* justification for using both top-down and bottom-up models even when these models produce different forecasts and state one justification for using the bottom-up approach by itself.

Murray suggests replacing earnings-based models with asset-based models in valuing equity markets. In response, McLean recommends using Tobin's q ratio and equity q ratio, although both are subject to estimation errors when applied to valuing a particular company.

D. Identify *two* problems that McLean may have in estimating the Tobin's q ratio and the equity q ratio for the pension plan assets that she manages.

Use the following information to answer Questions 3 through 10.

Claudia Atkinson, CFA, is chief economist of an investment management firm. In analyzing equity markets, the firm has always used a bottom-up approach but now Atkinson is in the process of implementing a top-down approach. She is discussing this topic with her assistant, Nicholas Ryan.

At Atkinson's request, Ryan has prepared a memo comparing the top-down approach and the bottom-up approach. Ryan presents three conclusions:

Conclusion 1: The top-down approach is less optimistic when the economy is heading into a recession than the bottom-up approach.
Conclusion 2: The top-down approach is more often based on consensus earnings estimates from equity analysts than the bottom-up approach.
Conclusion 3: The top-down approach is often more accurate in predicting the effect on the stock market of a contemporaneous change in a key economic variable than is the bottom-up approach.

Atkinson explains to Ryan how the Cobb-Douglas function can be used to model GDP growth under assumptions of constant returns to scale. For illustrative purposes, she uses the data shown in Exhibit C.

EXHIBIT C Hypothetical Data for a Developing Country

Time Period	Growth in Total Factor Productivity	Output Elasticity of Capital	Growth in Capital Stock	Growth in Labor Input
1970–1989	2.5%	0.4	4.8%	3.0%
1990–2009	2.8%	0.4	4.4%	4.6%

Atkinson wants to use the data shown in Exhibit C as an input for estimating justified P/E ratios. Ryan expresses some criticisms about using such historical data:

- "In a context of hyperinflation, the approach may not be appropriate."
- "The companies' growth rates may not match GDP growth for long periods."
- "Government-implemented measures may not be taken into account in any of the growth factors."

Atkinson intends to use relative value models in order to support the firm's asset allocation recommendation. The earnings-based approach that she studies is the Fed model. She asks Ryan to write a summary of the advantages of that model. Ryan's report makes the following assertions about the Fed model:

- "The model can be used for non-U.S. equity markets."
- "The model captures the net present value of growth investment opportunities available to investors."
- "The model is most informative when the excess of the earnings yield over the Treasury bond yield is close to the historical average."

Atkinson thinks that the Yardeni model might address some of the criticisms of the Fed model and bring certain improvements. She will use that model as an alternate approach.

Because different results from various equity market valuation models may provide relevant information, Atkinson will present a third earnings-based approach, namely the P/10-year MA(E) model. Ryan identifies many positive features in that model, including the following:

- "The model controls for inflation."
- "The model is independent of changes in accounting rules."
- "The model controls for business cycle effects on earnings."

When evaluating the equity market in the United States, Atkinson uses the following asset-based models: Tobin's q ratio and equity q ratio. She calculates the equity q ratio of Nonfarm Nonfinancial Corporate Business based on the Federal Reserve data shown in Exhibit D.

EXHIBIT D Nonfarm Nonfinancial Corporate Business for Fourth Quarter of 2008 (billions of U.S. dollars)

Assets at market value or replacement cost	27.3
Assets at book value	23.4
Liabilities	13.3
Equities at market value	9.0

Atkinson notes that the Tobin's q ratio that could be derived from Exhibit D is less than 1. She asks Ryan what conclusion could be drawn from such a low ratio if it had been obtained for a specific company.

3. Which conclusion presented by Ryan about the top-down approach and the bottom-up approach is *most likely* correct?

    A. Conclusion 1.
    B. Conclusion 2.
    C. Conclusion 3.

4. Based on Exhibit C, which of the components of economic growth has contributed most to GDP growth during the 1970–1989 time period?

    A. Labor input.
    B. Capital stock.
    C. Total factor productivity.

5. Which of the following criticisms expressed by Ryan about the use of historical data is the *least* valid?

    A. In a context of hyperinflation, the approach may not be appropriate.
    B. The companies' growth rates may not match GDP growth for long periods.
    C. Government-implemented measures may not be taken into account in any of the growth factors.

6. Which of the following advantages listed by Ryan with respect to the earnings-based approach studied by Atkinson is *most likely* correct? The model

    A. Can be used for non-U.S. equity markets.
    B. Captures the net present value of growth investment opportunities available to investors.
    C. Is most informative when the excess of the earnings yield over the Treasury bond yield is close to the historical average.

7. The *most likely* improvement from using the Yardeni model instead of the Fed model is that the Yardeni model captures:
   A. A pure equity risk premium.
   B. A pure default risk premium.
   C. The effect of long-term earnings growth on equity market values.
8. Which of the following features of the P/10-year MA(E) model as stated by Ryan is *least likely* to be correct? The model
   A. Controls for inflation.
   B. Is independent of changes in accounting rules.
   C. Controls for business cycle effects on earnings.
9. Based on the data shown in Exhibit D, the equity q ratio is closest to:
   A. 0.6429.
   B. 0.8168.
   C. 0.8911.
10. The best conclusion that Ryan can provide to Atkinson regarding the calculated value for Tobin's q ratio is that, based on comparing it to an equilibrium value of 1:
    A. The replacement cost of assets is understated.
    B. The company appears to be overvalued in the marketplace.
    C. The company appears to be undervalued in the marketplace.

Use the following information to answer Questions 11 through 16.

Egon Carmichael, CFA, is a senior analyst at Supranational Investment Management (Supranational), a firm specializing in global investment analysis. He is meeting with Nicolas Schmidt, a potential client representing a life insurance company, discussing a report prepared by Supranational on the U.S. equity market. The report contains valuations of the U.S. equity market based on two approaches: the justified P/E model and the Fed model.

When Carmichael informs Schmidt that Supranational applies the neoclassical approach to growth accounting, Schmidt makes the following statements about what he considers to be some limitations of that approach:

Statement 1: The growth in total factor productivity is not directly observable.
Statement 2: The growth factors must be stated in nominal (i.e., not inflation-adjusted) terms.
Statement 3: The total output may not grow at a rate faster than predicted by the growth in capital stock and in labor force.

For use in estimating the justified P/E based on the Gordon constant growth model, Carmichael develops the assumptions displayed in Exhibit E.

EXHIBIT E Justified P/E Ratio for the U.S. Equity Market: Assumptions

Required real rate of return	5.0%
Inflation-adjusted dividend growth rate	2.5%

Using these assumptions, Carmichael's estimate of the justified P/E ratio for the U.S. equity market is 13.2. Schmidt asks Carmichael, "All else equal, what would cause the justified P/E for the U.S. equity market to fall?"

Supranational's report concludes that the U.S. equity market is currently undervalued, based on the Fed model. Schmidt asks Carmichael, "Which of the following scenarios would result in the Fed model most likely indicating that the U.S. equity market is overvalued?"

Scenario 1: The S&P 500 forward earnings yield is 4.5 percent and the 10-year T-note yield is 4.75 percent.
Scenario 2: The S&P 500 forward earnings yield is 4.5 percent, the 10-year T-note yield is 4.0 percent, and the average difference between the S&P 500 forward earnings yield and the 10-year T-note over the last 20 years has been 0.25 percent.
Scenario 3: The long-term inflation rate is expected to be 2 percent and the long-term average earnings growth is expected to be 1 percent real.

Schmidt points out that the Fed model has been the subject of criticism and recommends that Carmichael use the Yardeni model to value the U.S. equity market. Before employing the Yardeni model, Carmichael asks Schmidt to identify criticisms of the Fed model that are addressed by the Yardeni model.

Finally, Carmichael presents a third earnings-based approach, the P/10-year MA(E) model, and describes many positive features of that model.

Schmidt mentions that the international life insurance company that he represents might be interested in the equity forecasts produced by Supranational. He says that his company's objective is to accumulate sufficient assets to fulfill the firm's obligations under its long term insurance and annuity contracts. For competitive reasons, the company wants to quickly detect significant cyclical turns in equity markets and to minimize tracking errors with respect to the equity index. Schmidt asks Carmichael to identify the forecasting approach that is most appropriate.

11. Which of the statements expressed by Schmidt about the neoclassical approach to growth accounting is correct?
    A. Statement 1.
    B. Statement 2.
    C. Statement 3.
12. Carmichael's *most appropriate* response to Schmidt's question about the justified P/E ratio is:
    A. Lower volatility of the U.S. equity market.
    B. Higher inflation-adjusted dividend growth rate.
    C. Higher correlation of U.S. equity market with international equity markets.
13. Carmichael's *most appropriate* response to Schmidt's question about the Fed model is:
    A. Scenario 1.
    B. Scenario 2.
    C. Scenario 3.
14. In response to Carmichael's question about which criticisms of the Fed model are addressed by the Yardeni model, Schmidt's *most appropriate* response is that the Yardeni model does take account of the criticism that the Fed model:
    A. Assumes that investors value earnings rather than dividends.
    B. Ignores long-term earnings growth opportunities available to shareholders.
    C. Assumes that the required rate of return on equity equals the Treasury bill rate.

15. Which of the following features is *least* applicable to the third earnings-based approach presented by Carmichael? The model:

    A. Controls for inflation.
    B. Is independent of changes in accounting rules.
    C. Controls for business cycle effects on earnings.

16. Carmichael's *best* answer to Schmidt's question about a recommended forecasting approach is to use:

    A. A top-down approach.
    B. A bottom-up approach.
    C. Both top-down and bottom-up approaches.

CHAPTER 12

TECHNICAL ANALYSIS

LEARNING OUTCOMES

After completing this chapter, you will be able to do the following:

- Explain the principles of technical analysis, its applications, and its underlying assumptions.
- Discuss the construction and interpretation of different types of technical analysis charts.
- Demonstrate the uses of trend, support and resistance lines, and change in polarity.
- Identify and interpret common chart patterns.
- Discuss common technical analysis indicators: price-based indicators, momentum oscillators, sentiment, and flow of funds.
- Explain the use of cycles by technical analysts.
- Discuss the key tenets of Elliott Wave Theory and the importance of Fibonacci numbers.
- Describe intermarket analysis as it relates to technical analysis and asset allocation.

SUMMARY OVERVIEW

- Technical analysis is a form of security analysis that uses price and volume market data, often graphically displayed.
- Technical analysis can be used for any freely traded security in the global market and is used on a wide range of financial instruments, such as equities, bonds, commodity futures, and currency futures.
- Technical analysis is the study of market trends or patterns and relies on recognition of patterns that have worked in the past in an attempt to predict future security prices. Technicians believe that market trends and patterns repeat themselves and are somewhat predictable because human behavior tends to repeat itself and is somewhat predictable.
- Another tenet of technical analysis is that the market brings together the collective wisdom of multiple participants, weights it according to the size of the trades they make, and allows analysts to understand this collective sentiment. Technical analysis relies on knowledgeable market participants putting this knowledge to work in the market and thereby influencing prices and volume.
- Technical analysis and fundamental analysis are equally useful and valid, but they approach the market in different ways. Technical analysis focuses solely on analyzing markets and the trading of financial instruments, whereas fundamental analysis is a much wider ranging field encompassing financial and economic analysis as well as analysis of societal and political trends.

- Technical analysis relies primarily on information gathered from market participants that is expressed through the interaction of price and volume. Fundamental analysis relies on information that is external to the market (e.g., economic data, company financial information) in an attempt to evaluate a security's value relative to its current price.
- The usefulness of technical analysis is diminished by any constraints on the security being freely traded, by large outside manipulation of the market, and in illiquid markets.
- Charts provide information about past price behavior and provide a basis for inferences about likely future price behavior. Various types of charts can be useful in studying the markets: line charts, bar charts, candlestick charts, and point and figure charts.
- Relative strength analysis is based on the ratio of the prices of a security to a benchmark and is used to compare the performance of one asset with the performance of another asset.
- Many technicians consider volume information to be very important and watch for the confirmation in volume of a price trend or the divergence of volume from a price trend.
- The concept of trend is perhaps the most important aspect of technical analysis. An uptrend is defined as a security making higher highs and higher lows. To draw an uptrend line, a technician draws a line connecting the lows of the price chart. A downtrend is defined as a security making lower highs and lower lows. To draw a downtrend line, a technician draws a line connecting the highs of the price chart.
- Support is defined as a low price range in which the price stops declining because of buying activity. It is the opposite of resistance, which is a price range in which price stops rising because of selling activity.
- Chart patterns are formations appearing in price charts that create some type of recognizable shape.
- Reversal patterns signal the end of a trend. Common reversal patterns are the head and shoulders, the inverse head and shoulders, double tops and bottoms, and triple tops and bottoms.
- Continuation patterns indicate that a market trend in place prior to the pattern formation will continue once the pattern is completed. Common continuation patterns are triangles, rectangles, flags, and pennants.
- Price-based indicators incorporate information contained in market prices. Common price-based indicators are the moving average and Bollinger Bands.
- Momentum oscillator indicators are constructed from price data, but they are calculated so that they fluctuate either between a high and low, typically 0 and 100, or around 0 or 100. Some examples are momentum (or rate of change) oscillators, the RSI, stochastic measures, and MACD.
- Sentiment indicators attempt to gauge investor activity for signs of increasing bullishness or bearishness. Sentiment indicators come in two forms—investor polls and calculated statistical indices. Opinion polls to gauge investors' sentiment toward the equity market are conducted by a variety of services. Commonly used calculated statistical indices are the put/call ratio, the VIX, margin debt, and the short interest ratio.
- Flow-of-funds indicators help technicians gauge potential changes in supply and demand for securities. Some commonly used indicators are the ARMS Index (also called the TRIN), margin debt (also a sentiment indicator), mutual fund cash positions, new equity issuance, and secondary equity offerings.
- Many technicians use various observed cycles to predict future movements in security prices; these cycles include Kondratieff waves, decennial patterns, and the U.S. presidential cycle.

- Elliott Wave Theory is an approach to market forecasting that assumes that markets form repetitive wave patterns, which are themselves composed of smaller and smaller subwaves. The relationships among wave heights are frequently Fibonacci ratios.
- Intermarket analysis is based on the principle that all markets are interrelated and influence each other. This approach involves the use of relative strength analysis for different groups of securities (e.g., stocks versus bonds, sectors in an economy, and securities from different countries) to make allocation decisions.

PROBLEMS

1. Technical analysis relies most importantly on:
   A. Price and volume data.
   B. Accurate financial statements.
   C. Fundamental analysis to confirm conclusions.

2. Which of the following is *not* an assumption of technical analysis?
   A. Security markets are efficient.
   B. The security under analysis is freely traded.
   C. Market trends and patterns tend to repeat themselves.

3. Drawbacks of technical analysis include which of the following?
   A. It identifies changes in trends only after the fact.
   B. Deviations from intrinsic value can persist for long periods.
   C. It usually requires detailed knowledge of the financial instrument under analysis.

4. Why is technical analysis especially useful in the analysis of commodities and currencies?
   A. Government regulators are more likely to intervene in these markets.
   B. These types of securities display clearer trends than equities and bonds do.
   C. Valuation models cannot be used to determine fundamental intrinsic value for these securities.

5. A daily bar chart provides:
   A. A logarithmically scaled horizontal axis.
   B. A horizontal axis that represents changes in price.
   C. High and low prices during the day and the day's opening and closing prices.

6. A candlestick chart is similar to a bar chart *except* that the candlestick chart:
   A. Represents upward movements in price with X's.
   B. Also graphically shows the range of the period's highs and lows.
   C. Has a body that is light or dark depending on whether the security closed higher or lower than its open.

7. In analyzing a price chart, high or increasing volume *most likely* indicates which of the following?
   A. Predicts a reversal in the price trend.
   B. Predicts that a trendless period will follow.
   C. Confirms a rising or declining trend in prices.

8. In constructing a chart, using a logarithmic scale on the vertical axis is likely to be *most useful* for which of the following applications?
   A. The price of gold for the past 100 years.
   B. The share price of a company over the past month.
   C. Yields on 10-year U.S. Treasuries for the past five years.

9. A downtrend line is constructed by drawing a line connecting:
   A. The lows of the price chart.
   B. The highs of the price chart.
   C. The highest high to the lowest low of the price chart.

10. The following exhibit depicts GreatWall Information Industry Co., Ltd., ordinary shares, traded on the Shenzhen Stock Exchange, for late 2008 through late 2009 in renminbi (RMB).

CANDLESTICK CHART GreatWall Information Industry Co., Ltd. Price Data, November 2008–September 2009 (price measured in RMB × 100)

Based on this chart, the uptrend was *most likely* broken at a level nearest to:
   A. 7 RMB.
   B. 8.5 RMB.
   C. 10 RMB.

11. The "change in polarity" principle states which of the following?
   A. Once an uptrend is broken, it becomes a downtrend.
   B. Once a resistance level is breached, it becomes a support level.
   C. The short-term moving average has crossed over the longer-term moving average.

12. The following exhibit depicts Barclays ordinary shares, traded on the London Stock Exchange, for 2009 in British pence.

CANDLESTICK CHART Barclays PLC Price Data, January 2009–January 2010 (price measured in British pence)

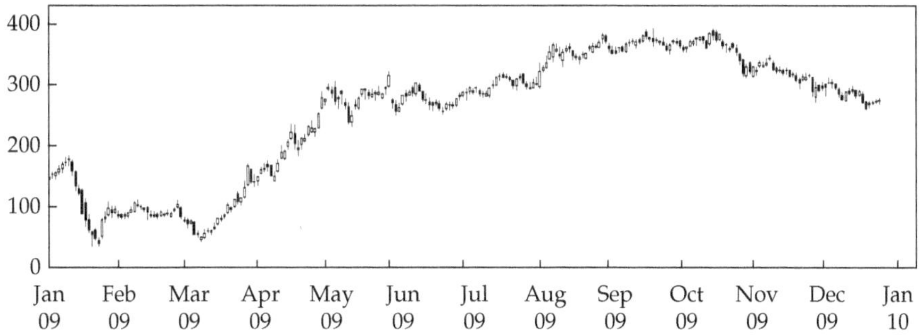

Based on this chart, Barclays appears to show resistance at a level nearest to:

A. 50p.
B. 275p.
C. 390p.

13. The following exhibit depicts Archer Daniels Midland Company common shares, traded on the New York Stock Exchange, for 1996 to 2001 in U.S. dollars.

CANDLESTICK CHART Archer Daniels Midland Company, February 1996–February 2001

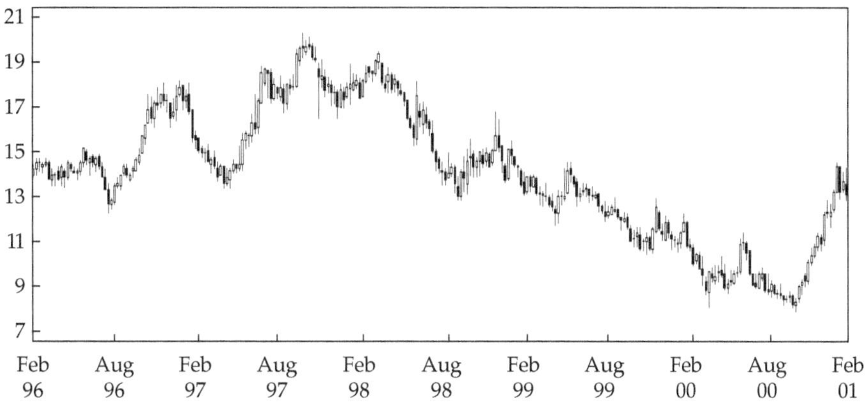

This chart illustrates *most* clearly which type of pattern?

A. Triangle.
B. Triple top.
C. Head and shoulders.

14. In an inverted head and shoulders pattern, if the neckline is at €100, the shoulders at €90, and the head at €75, the price target is *closest* to which of the following?
    A. €50.
    B. €110.
    C. €125.

15. Which flow-of-funds indicator is considered bearish for equities?
    A. A large increase in the number of IPOs.
    B. Higher-than-average cash balances in mutual funds.
    C. An upturn in margin debt but one that is still below the long-term average.

16. A TRIN with a value of less than 1.0 indicates:
    A. The market is in balance.
    B. There is more volume in rising shares.
    C. There is more volume in declining shares.

17. Bollinger Bands are constructed by plotting:
    A. A MACD line and a signal line.
    B. A moving-average line with an uptrend line above and downtrend line below.
    C. A moving-average line with upper and lower lines that are at a set number of standard deviations apart.

18. Which of the following is *not* a momentum oscillator?
    A. MACD.
    B. Stochastic oscillator.
    C. Bollinger Bands.

19. Which of the following is a continuation pattern?
    A. Triangle.
    B. Triple top.
    C. Head and shoulders.

20. Which of the following is a reversal pattern?
    A. Pennant.
    B. Rectangle.
    C. Double bottom.

21. Which of the following is generally true of the head and shoulders pattern?
    A. Volume is important in interpreting the data.
    B. The neckline, once breached, becomes a support level.
    C. Head and shoulders patterns are generally followed by an uptrend in the security's price.

22. Nikolai Kondratieff concluded in the 1920s that since the 1780s, Western economies have generally followed a cycle of how many years?
    A. 18.
    B. 54.
    C. 76.

23. Based on the decennial pattern of cycles, how would the return of the Dow Jones Industrial Average (DJIA) in the year 2015 compare with the return in 2020?
    A. The return would be better.
    B. The return would be worse.
    C. The answer cannot be determined because the theory does not apply to both of those years.

24. According to the U.S. presidential cycle theory, the DJIA has the best performance during which year?
    A. The presidential election year itself.
    B. The first year following a presidential election.
    C. The third year following a presidential election.

25. What is a major problem with long-term cycle theories?
    A. The sample size is small.
    B. The data are usually hard to observe.
    C. They occur over such a long period that they are difficult to discern.

26. In 1938, R.N. Elliott proposed a theory that equity markets move:
    A. In stochastic waves.
    B. In cycles following Fibonacci ratios.
    C. In waves dependent on other securities.

27. All of the following are names of Elliott cycles *except*:
    A. Presidential.
    B. Supercycle.
    C. Grand supercycle.

28. To identify intermarket relationships, technicians commonly use:
    A. Stochastic oscillators.
    B. Fibonacci ratios.
    C. Relative strength analysis.

PART II

SOLUTIONS

CHAPTER 1

MARKET ORGANIZATION AND STRUCTURE

SOLUTIONS

1. C is correct. Takabe is best characterized as an information-motivated trader. Takabe believes that his model provides him superior information about the movements in the stock market and his motive for trading is to profit from this information.
2. B is correct. Beach is an investor. He is simply investing in risky assets consistent with his level of risk aversion. Beach is not hedging any existing risk or using information to identify and trade mispriced securities. Therefore, he is not a hedger or an information-motivated trader.
3. A is correct. Smith is a hedger. The short position on the BRL futures contract offsets the BRL long position in three months. She is hedging the risk of the BRL depreciating against the USD. If the BRL depreciates, the value of the cash inflow goes down in USD terms but there is a gain on the futures contracts.
4. A is correct. Regulation of arbitrageurs' profits is not a function of the financial system. The financial system facilitates the allocation of capital to the best uses and the purposes for which people use the financial system, including borrowing money.
5. C is correct. The purchase of real estate properties is a transaction in the alternative investment market.
6. B is correct. The 90-day commercial paper and negotiable certificates of deposit are money market instruments.
7. B is correct. This transaction is a sale in the primary market. It is a sale of shares from the issuer to the investor and funds flow to the issuer of the security from the purchaser.
8. A is correct. Warrants are *least likely* to be part of the fund. Warrant holders have the right to buy the issuer's common stock. Thus, warrants are typically classified as equity and are least likely to be a part of a fixed-income mutual fund. Commercial paper and repurchase agreements are short-term fixed-income securities.
9. C is correct. When investors want to sell their shares, investors of an open-end fund sell the shares back to the fund whereas investors of a closed-end fund sell the shares to others in the secondary market. Closed-end funds are available to new investors but they must purchase shares in the fund in the secondary market. The shares of a closed-end fund trade at a premium or discount to net asset value.

10. A is correct. Once you have entered into a forward contract, it is difficult to exit from the contract. As opposed to a futures contract, trading out of a forward contract is quite difficult. There is no exchange of cash at the origination of a forward contract. There is no exchange on a forward contract until the maturity of the contract.
11. A is correct. Harris is least likely to find counterparty risk associated with a futures contract. There is limited counterparty risk in a futures contract because the clearinghouse is on the other side of every contract.
12. B is correct. Buying a put option on the dollar will ensure a minimum exchange rate but does not have to be exercised if the exchange rate moves in a favorable direction. Forward and futures contracts would lock in a fixed rate but would not allow for the possibility to profit in case the value of the dollar three months later in the spot market turns out to be greater than the value in the forward or futures contract.
13. B is correct. The agreement between the publisher and the paper supplier to respectively buy and supply paper in the future at a price agreed upon today is a forward contract.
14. B is correct. SPDRs trade in the secondary market and are a pooled investment vehicle.
15. B is correct. The holder of the call option will exercise the call options if the price is above the exercise price of \$120 per share. Note that if the stock price is above \$120 but less than \$123, the option would be exercised even though the net result for the option buyer after considering the premium is a loss. For example, if the stock price is \$122, the option buyer would exercise the option to make \$2 = \$122 − \$120 per share, resulting in a loss of \$1 = \$3 − \$2 after considering the premium. It is better to exercise and have a loss of only \$1, however, than not to exercise and lose the entire \$3 premium.
16. B is correct. The investment companies that create exchange-traded funds (ETFs) are financial intermediaries. ETFs are securities that represent ownership in the assets held by the fund. The transaction costs of trading shares of ETFs are substantially lower than the combined costs of trading the underlying assets of the ETF.
17. B is correct. The process can best be described as arbitrage because it involves buying and selling instruments, whose values are closely related, at different prices in different markets.
18. A is correct. Robert's exposure to the risk of the stock of the Michelin Group is long. The exposure as a result of the long call position is long. The exposure as a result of the short put position is also long. Therefore, the combined exposure is long.
19. B is correct. The maximum leverage ratio is 1.82 = 100% position ÷ 55% equity. The maximum leverage ratio associated with a position financed by the minimum margin requirement is one divided by the minimum margin requirement.
20. C is correct. The return is 50 percent. If the position had been unleveraged, the return would be 20% = (60 − 50)/50. Because of leverage, the return is 50% = 2.5 × 20%.

    Another way to look at this problem is that the equity contributed by the trader (the minimum margin requirement) is 40% = 100% ÷ 2.5. The trader contributed \$20 = 40% of \$50 per share. The gain is \$10 per share, resulting in a return of 50% = 10/20.
21. B is correct. The return is −15.4 percent.

    Total cost of the purchase = \$16,000 = 500 × \$32
    Equity invested = \$12,000 = 0.75 × \$16,000
    Amount borrowed = \$4,000 = 16,000 − 12,000
    Interest paid at month end = \$80 = 0.02 × \$4,000
    Dividend received at month end = \$250 = 500 × \$0.50
    Proceeds on stock sale = \$14,000 = 500 × \$28

PART II

SOLUTIONS

Total commissions paid = \$20 = \$10 + \$10
Net gain/loss = −\$1,850 = −16,000 − 80 + 250 + 14,000 − 20
Initial investment including commission on purchase = \$12,010
Return = −15.4% = −\$1,850/\$12,010

22. A is correct. She will need to contribute €3,760 as margin. In view of the possibility of a loss, if the stock price goes up, she will need to contribute €3,760 = 40% of €9,400 as the initial margin. Rogers will need to leave the proceeds from the short sale (€9,400 = 200 × €47) on deposit.
23. B is correct. A margin call will first occur at a price of \$17.86. Because you have contributed half and borrowed the remaining half, your initial equity is 50 percent of the initial stock price, or \$12.50 = 0.50 × \$25. If P is the subsequent price, your equity would change by an amount equal to the change in price. So, your equity at price P would be 12.50 + (P − 25). A margin call will occur when the percentage margin drops to 30 percent. So, the price at which a margin call will occur is the solution to the following equation.

$$\frac{\text{Equity/Share}}{\text{Price/Share}} = \frac{12.50 + P - 25}{P} = 30\%$$

The solution is P = \$17.86.

24. B is correct. An instruction regarding when to fill an order is considered a validity instruction.
25. C is correct. The market is 9.95 bid, offered at 10.02. The best bid is at €9.95 and the best offer is €10.02.
26. C is correct. This order is said to make a new market. The new buy order is at ¥123.40, which is better than the current best bid of ¥123.35. Therefore, the buy order is making a new market. Had the new order been at ¥123.35, it would be said to make the market. Because the new buy limit order is at a price less than the best offer of ¥123.80, it will not immediately execute and is not taking the market.
27. A is correct. This order is said to take the market. The new sell order is at \$54.62, which is at the current best bid. Therefore, the new sell order will immediately trade with the current best bid and is taking the market.
28. B is correct. The maximum possible loss is \$1,300. If the stock price crosses \$50, the stop buy order will become valid and will get executed at a maximum limit price of \$55. The maximum loss per share is \$13 = \$55 − \$42, or \$1,300 for 100 shares.
29. B is correct. The most appropriate order is a good-till-cancelled stop sell order. This order will be acted on if the stock price declines below a specified price (in this case, \$27.50). This order is sometimes referred to as a good-till-cancelled stop loss sell order. You are generally bullish about the stock, as indicated by no immediate intent to sell, and would expect a loss on short selling the stock. A stop buy order is placed to buy a stock when the stock is going up.
30. B is correct. The investment bank bears the risk that the issue may be undersubscribed at the offering price. If the entire issue is not sold, the investment bank underwriting the issue will buy the unsold securities at the offering price.
31. B is correct. This sale is a private placement. As the company is already publicly traded, the share sale is clearly not an initial public offering. The sale also does not involve a shelf registration because the company is not selling shares to the public on a piecemeal basis.

32. A is correct. This offering is a rights offering. The company is distributing rights to buy stock at a fixed price to existing shareholders in proportion to their holdings.
33. C is correct. Order III (time of arrival of 9:53:04) has precedence. In the order precedence hierarchy, the first rule is price priority. Based on this rule, sell orders II, III, and IV get precedence over order I. The next rule is display precedence at a given price. Because order II is a hidden order, orders III and IV get precedence. Finally, order III gets precedence over order IV based on time priority at same price and same display status.
34. C is correct. The order for 500 shares would get cancelled; there would be no fill. Li is willing to buy at CNY 74.25 or less but the minimum offer price in the book is CNY 74.30, therefore, no part of the order would be filled. Because Li's order is immediate-or-cancel, it would be cancelled.
35. B is correct. Ian's average trade price is:

$$\pounds 19.92 = \frac{300 \times \pounds 20.02 + 400 \times \pounds 19.89 + 200 \times \pounds 19.84}{300 + 400 + 200}$$

Ian's sell order first fills with the most aggressively priced buy order, which is Mary's order for 300 shares at £20.02. Ian still has 700 shares for sale. The next most aggressively priced buy order is Ann's order for 400 shares at £19.89. This order is filled. Ian still has 300 shares for sale. The next most aggressively priced buy order is Paul's order for 200 shares at £19.84. A third trade takes place. Ian still has 100 shares for sale.

The next buy order is Keith's order for 1,000 shares at £19.70. However, this price is below Ian's limit price of £19.83. Therefore, no more trade is possible.
36. C is correct. In such a market, well-informed traders will find it easy to trade and their trading will make the market more informationally efficient. In a liquid market, it is easier for informed traders to fill their orders. Their trading will cause prices to incorporate their information and the prices will be more in line with the fundamental values.
37. C is correct. Ensuring that investors in the stock market achieve a rate of return that is at least equal to the risk-free rate of return is least likely to be included as an objective of market regulation. Stocks are risky investments and there would be occasions when a stock market investment would not only have a return less than the risk-free rate but also a negative return. Minimizing agency costs and ensuring that financial markets are fair and orderly are objectives of market regulation.

CHAPTER 2

SECURITY MARKET INDICES

SOLUTIONS

1. C is correct. A security market index represents the value of a given security market, market segment, or asset class.
2. A is correct. Security market indices are constructed and managed like a portfolio of securities.
3. A is correct. The first decision is identifying the target market that the index is intended to represent because the target market determines the investment universe and the securities available for inclusion in the index.
4. C is correct. The difference between a price return index and a total return index consisting of identical securities and weights is the income generated over time by the underlying securities. If the securities in the index do not generate income, both indices will be identical in value.
5. A is correct. At inception, the values of the price return and total return versions of an index are equal.
6. B is correct. The price return is the sum of the weighted returns of each security. The return of Able is 20 percent [(12 − 10)/10]; of Baker is −5 percent [(19 − 20)/20]; and of Charlie is 0 percent [(30 − 30)/30]. The price return index assigns a weight of 1/3 to each asset; therefore, the price return is 1/3 × [20% + (−5%) + 0%] = 5%.
7. C is correct. The total return of an index is calculated on the basis of the change in price of the underlying securities plus the sum of income received or the sum of the weighted total returns of each security. The total return of Able is 27.5 percent; of Baker is 0 percent; and of Charlie is 6.7 percent:
   Able: (12 − 10 + 0.75)/10 = 27.5%
   Baker: (19 − 20 + 1)/20 = 0%
   Charlie: (30 − 30 + 2)/30 = 6.7%
   An equal-weighted index applies the same weight (1/3) to each security's return; therefore, the total return = 1/3 × (27.5% + 0% + 6.7%) = 11.4%.
8. B is correct. The price return of the price-weighted index is the percentage change in price of the index: (68 − 75)/75 = −9.33%.

Security	Beginning of Period Price £	End of Period Price £
ABC	25.00	27.00
DEF	35.00	25.00
GHI	15.00	16.00
TOTAL	75.00	68.00

9. B is correct. The price return of the index is (48,250,000 − 53,750,000)/53,750,000 = −10.23%.

Security	Beginning of Period Price ¥	Shares Outstanding	Beginning of Period Value ¥	End of Period Price ¥	End of Period Value ¥
MNO	2,500	5,000	12,500,000	2,700	13,500,000
QRS	3,500	7,500	26,250,000	2,500	18,750,000
XYZ	1,500	10,000	15,000,000	1,600	16,000,000
Total			53,750,000		48,250,000

10. B is correct. The total return of the market-capitalization-weighted index is calculated below:

Security	Beginning of Period Value ¥	End of Period Value ¥	Total Dividends ¥	Total Return %
MNO	12,500,000	13,500,000	500,000	12.00
QRS	26,250,000	18,750,000	1,125,000	−24.29
XYZ	15,000,000	16,000,000	1,000,000	13.33
Total	53,750,000	48,250,000	2,625,000	−5.35

11. A is correct. The target market determines the investment universe and the securities available for inclusion in the index.
12. A is correct. The sum of prices at the beginning of the period is 96; the sum at the end of the period is 100. Regardless of the divisor, the price return is 100/96 − 1 = 0.042 or 4.2 percent.
13. B is correct. It is the percentage change in the market value over the period:
Market value at beginning of period: (20 × 300) + (50 × 300) + (26 × 2,000) = 73,000
Market value at end of period: (22 × 300) + (48 × 300) + (30 × 2,000) = 81,000
Percentage change is 81,000/73,000 − 1 = 0.1096 or 11.0 percent with rounding.
14. C is correct. With an equal-weighted index, the same amount is invested in each security. Assuming $1,000 is invested in each of the three stocks, the index value is $3,000 at the beginning of the period and the following number of shares is purchased for each stock:
Security A: 50 shares
Security B: 20 shares
Security C: 38.46 shares.

    Using the prices at the beginning of the period for each security, the index value at the end of the period is $3,213.8: ($22 × 50) + ($48 × 20) + ($30 × 38.46). The price return is $3,213.8/$3,000 − 1 = 7.1%.
15. A is correct. In the price-weighting method, the divisor must be adjusted so the index value immediately after the split is the same as the index value immediately prior to the split.

16. C is correct. The main source of return differences arises from outperformance of small-cap securities or underperformance of large-cap securities. In an equal-weighted index, securities that constitute the largest fraction of the market are underrepresented and securities that constitute only a small fraction of the market are overrepresented. Thus, higher equal-weighted index returns will occur if the smaller-cap equities outperform the larger-cap equities.
17. C is correct. "Float" is the number of shares available for public trading.
18. B is correct. Fundamental weighting leads to indices that have a value tilt.
19. C is correct. Rebalancing refers to adjusting the weights of constituent securities in an index to maintain consistency with the index's weighting method.
20. B is correct. Changing market prices will cause weights that were initially equal to become unequal, thus requiring rebalancing.
21. C is correct. Reconstitution is the process by which index providers review the constituent securities, reapply the initial criteria for inclusion in the index, and select which securities to retain, remove, or add. Constituent securities that no longer meet the criteria are replaced with securities that do. Thus, reconstitution reduces the likelihood that the index includes securities that are not representative of the target market.
22. C is correct. Security market indices play a critical role as proxies for asset classes in asset allocation models.
23. A is correct. Security market indices are used as proxies for measuring market or systematic risk, not as measures of systematic risk.
24. B is correct. Sector indices provide a means to determine whether a portfolio manager is more successful at stock selection or sector allocation.
25. C is correct. Style indices represent groups of securities classified according to market capitalization, value, growth, or a combination of these characteristics.
26. A is correct. The large number of fixed-income securities—combined with the lack of liquidity of some securities—makes it costly and difficult for investors to replicate fixed-income indices.
27. C is correct. An aggregate fixed-income index can be subdivided by market sector (government, government agency, collateralized, corporate), style (maturity, credit quality), economic sector, or some other characteristic to create more narrowly defined indices.
28. C is correct. Coupon frequency is not a dimension on which fixed-income indices are based.
29. A is correct. Commodity indices consist of futures contracts on one or more commodities.
30. C is correct. The performance of commodity indices can be quite different from that of the underlying commodities because the indices consist of futures contracts on the commodities rather than the actual commodities.
31. B is correct. It is not a real estate index category.
32. B is correct. Hedge funds are not required to report their performance to any party other than their investors. Therefore, each hedge fund decides to which database(s) it will report its performance. Thus, for a hedge fund index, constituents determine the index rather than index providers determining the constituents.
33. A is correct. Voluntary performance reporting may lead to survivorship bias, and poorer performing hedge funds will be less likely to report their performance.
34. C is correct. The fixed-income market has more issuers and securities than the equity market.

CHAPTER 3

MARKET EFFICIENCY

SOLUTIONS

1. C is correct. Today's price change is independent of the one from yesterday, and in an efficient market, investors will react to new, independent information as it is made public.
2. A is correct. Reducing the number of market participants can accentuate market imperfections and impede market efficiency (e.g., restrictions on foreign investor trading).
3. A is correct. According to theory, reducing the restrictions on trading will allow for more arbitrage trading, thereby promoting more efficient pricing. Although regulators argue that short selling exaggerates downward price movements, empirical research indicates that short selling is helpful in price discovery.
4. C is correct. Regulation to restrict unfair use of nonpublic information encourages greater participation in the market, which increases market efficiency. Regulators (e.g., U.S. SEC) discourage illegal insider trading by issuing penalties to violators of their insider trading rules.
5. A is correct. Restricting short selling will reduce arbitrage trading, which promotes market efficiency. By contrast, allowing unrestricted foreign investor trading increases market participation, which makes markets more efficient. Furthermore, penalizing insider trading encourages greater market participation, which increases market efficiency.
6. B is correct. A security's intrinsic value and market value should be equal when markets are efficient.
7. B is correct. The intrinsic value of an undervalued asset is greater than the market value of the asset, where the market value is the transaction price at which an asset can be currently bought or sold.
8. B is correct. The market value is the transaction price at which an asset can be currently bought or sold.
9. A is correct. The weak-form efficient market hypothesis is defined as a market where security prices fully reflect all market data, which refers to all past price and trading volume information.
10. B is correct. In semistrong-form efficient markets, security prices reflect all publicly available information.
11. B is correct. If all public information should already be reflected in the market price, then the abnormal trading profit will be equal to zero when fundamental analysis is used.
12. B is correct. The strong-form efficient market hypothesis assumes all information, public or private, has already been reflected in the prices.

13. B is correct. Costs associated with active trading strategies would be difficult to recover; thus, such active trading strategies would have difficulty outperforming passive strategies on a consistent after-cost basis.
14. B is correct. In a semistrong-form efficient market, passive portfolio strategies should outperform active portfolio strategies on a risk-adjusted basis.
15. B is correct. Technical analysts use past prices and volume to predict future prices, which is inconsistent with the weakest form of market efficiency (i.e., weak-form market efficiency). Weak-form market efficiency states that investors cannot earn abnormal returns by trading on the basis of past trends in price and volume.
16. C is correct. Fundamental analysts use publicly available information to estimate a security's intrinsic value to determine if the security is mispriced, which is inconsistent with the semistrong form of market efficiency. Semistrong-form market efficiency states that investors cannot earn abnormal returns by trading based on publicly available information.
17. C is correct. If markets are not semistrong-form efficient, then fundamental analysts are able to use publicly available information to estimate a security's intrinsic value and identify misvalued securities. Technical analysis is not able to earn abnormal returns if markets are weak-form efficient. Passive portfolio managers outperform fundamental analysis if markets are semistrong-form efficient.
18. A is correct. Operating inefficiencies reduce market efficiency.
19. C is correct. If markets are efficient, the information from the annual report is reflected in the stock prices; therefore, the gradual changes must be from the release of additional information.
20. B is correct. The excess returns in January are not attributed to any new information or news; however, research has found that part of the seasonal pattern can be explained by tax-loss selling and portfolio window dressing.
21. A is correct. Finding significant abnormal returns does not necessarily indicate that markets are inefficient or that abnormal returns can be realized by applying the strategy to future time periods. Abnormal returns are considered market anomalies because they may be the result of the model used to estimate the expected returns or may be the result of underestimating transaction costs or other expenses associated with implementing the strategy, rather than because of market inefficiency.
22. B is correct. Trading based on historical momentum indicates that price patterns exist and can be exploited by using historical price information. A momentum trading strategy that produces abnormal returns contradicts the weak form of the efficient market hypothesis, which states that investors cannot earn abnormal returns on the basis of past trends in prices.
23. A is correct. Higher than average dividend yield is a characteristic of a value stock, along with low price-to-earnings and low market-to-book ratios. Growth stocks are characterized by low dividend yields and high price-to-earnings and high market-to-book ratios.
24. A is correct. The efficient market hypothesis and asset-pricing models only require that the market is rational. Behavioral finance is used to explain *some* of the market anomalies as irrational decisions.
25. B is correct. Behavioral theories of loss aversion can explain observed overreaction in markets, such that investors dislike losses more than comparable gains (i.e., risk is not symmetrical).
26. C is correct. Behavioral theories of loss aversion allow for the possibility that the dislike for risk is not symmetrical, which allows for loss aversion to explain observed overreaction in markets such that investors dislike losses more than they like comparable gains.

CHAPTER 4

PORTFOLIO MANAGEMENT: AN OVERVIEW

SOLUTIONS

1. A is correct. Combining assets into a portfolio should reduce the portfolio's volatility. Specifically, "individuals and institutions should hold portfolios to reduce risk." As illustrated in the reading, however, risk reduction may not be as great during a period of dramatic economic change.
2. A is correct. Combining assets into a portfolio should reduce the portfolio's volatility. The portfolio approach does not necessarily provide downside protection or guarantee that the portfolio always will avoid losses.
3. B is correct. As illustrated in the reading, portfolios reduce risk more than they increase returns.
4. A is correct. The excess reserves invested by banks need to be relatively liquid. Although investment companies and non-life insurance companies have high liquidity needs, the liquidity need for banks is on average the greatest.
5. B is correct. Most foundations and endowments are established with the intent of having perpetual lives. Although defined benefit plans and life insurance companies have portfolios with a long time horizon, they are not perpetual.
6. A is correct. Income is necessary to meet the cash flow obligation to retirees. Although defined benefit plans have a need for income, the need for liquidity typically is quite low. A retiree may need life insurance; however, a defined benefit plan does not need insurance.
7. B is correct. Investment companies manage investments in mutual funds. Although endowments and insurance companies may own mutual funds, they do not issue or redeem shares of mutual funds.
8. C is correct. The client's objectives and constraints are established in the investment policy statement and are used to determine the client's target asset allocation, which occurs in the execution step of the portfolio management process.
9. A is correct. Securities are analyzed in the execution step. In the planning step, a client's objectives and constraints are used to develop the investment policy statement.

10. B is correct. Portfolio monitoring and rebalancing occurs in the feedback step of the portfolio management process.
11. C is correct. Portfolio 3 has the same equity exposure as Portfolio 1 and has a higher exposure to alternative assets, which have greater volatility (as discussed in the readings comparing the endowments from Yale University and the University of Virginia).
12. B is correct. Open-end funds trade at their net asset value per share, whereas closed-end funds and exchange-traded funds can trade at a premium or a discount.
13. A is correct. Exchange-traded funds do not have capital gain distributions. If an investor sells shares of an ETF (or open-end mutual fund or closed-end mutual fund), the investor may have a capital gain or loss on the shares sold; however, the gain (or loss) from the sale is not a distribution.
14. A is correct. Hedge funds are currently exempt from the reporting requirements of a typical public investment company.
15. B is correct. Buyout funds or private equity firms make only a few large investments in private companies with the intent of selling the restructured companies in three to five years. Venture capital funds also have a short time horizon; however, these funds consist of many small investments in companies with the expectation that only a few will have a large payoff (and that most will fail).

CHAPTER 5

PORTFOLIO RISK AND RETURN: PART I

SOLUTIONS

1. C is correct. –10.1% is the holding period return, which is calculated as: (3,050 – 3,450 + 51.55)/3,450, which is composed of a dividend yield of 1.49% = 51.55/(3,450) and a capital loss yield of –11.59% = −400/(3,450).
2. B is correct. [(1 + 0.14)(1 − 0.10)(1 − 0.02)] − 1 = 0.0055 = 0.55%.
3. A is correct. $[(1 + 0.22)(1 - 0.25)(1 + 0.11)]^{(1/3)} - 1 = 1.0157^{(1/3)} - 1 = 0.0052 =$ 0.52%
4. A is correct. The geometric mean return compounds the returns instead of the amount invested.
5. B is correct. The annualized rate of return for ETF 2 is $12.05\% = (1.0110^{52/5}) - 1$, which is greater than the annualized rate of ETF 1, $11.93\% = (1.0461^{365/146}) - 1$, and ETF 3, $11.32\% = (1.1435^{12/15}) - 1$. Despite having the lowest value for the periodic rate, ETF 2 has the highest annualized rate of return because of the reinvestment rate assumption and the compounding of the periodic rate.
6. A is correct. The asset's returns are not used to calculate the portfolio's variance [only the assets' weights, standard deviations (or variances) and covariances (or correlations) are used].
7. C is correct.

$$\begin{aligned}\sigma_{port} &= \sqrt{w_1^2\sigma_1^2 + w_2^2\sigma_2^2 + 2w_1w_2\rho_{1,2}\sigma_1\sigma_2} \\ &= \sqrt{(0.3)^2(20\%)^2 + (0.7)^2(12\%)^2 + 2(0.3)(0.7)(0.40)(20\%)(12\%)} \\ &= (0.3600\% + 0.7056\% + 0.4032\%)^{0.5} = (1.4688\%)^{0.5} = 12.11\%.\end{aligned}$$

8. A is correct.

$$\begin{aligned}\sigma_{port} &= \sqrt{w_1^2\sigma_1^2 + w_2^2\sigma_2^2 + 2w_1w_2Cov(R_1R_2)} \\ &= \sqrt{(0.3)^2(20\%)^2 + (0.7)^2(12\%)^2 + 2(0.3)(0.7)(-0.0240)} \\ &= (0.3600\% + 0.7056\% - 1.008\%)^{0.5} = (0.0576\%)^{0.5} = 2.40\%.\end{aligned}$$

9. C is correct. A portfolio standard deviation of 14.40% is the weighted average, which is possible only if the correlation between the securities is equal to 1.0.

10. B is correct. A portfolio standard deviation of 14.40% is the weighted average, which is possible only if the correlation between the securities is equal to 1.0. If the correlation coefficient is equal to 1.0, then the covariance must equal 0.0240, calculated as: $\text{Cov}(R_1, R_2) = \rho_{12}\sigma_1\sigma_2 = (1.0)(20\%)(12\%) = 2.40\% = 0.0240$.
11. B is correct. (1 + 0.080)/(1 + 0.0210) = 5.8%.
12. A is correct. (1 + 0.065)/(1 + 0.0210) = 4.3%.
13. A is correct. (1 + 0.080)/(1 + 0.0250) = 5.4%.
14. B is correct. (1 + 0.0650)/(1 + 0.0250) = 3.9%.
15. C is correct. Brokerage commissions are negotiated with the brokerage firm. A security's liquidity impacts the operational efficiency of trading costs. Specifically, liquidity impacts the bid-ask spread and can impact the stock price (if the ability to sell the stock is impaired by the uncertainty associated with being able to sell the stock).
16. C is correct. Historical data over long periods of time indicate that there exists a positive risk–return relationship, which is a reflection of an investor's risk aversion.
17. A is correct. A risk-free asset has a variance of zero and is not dependent on whether the investor is risk-neutral, risk-seeking, or risk-averse. That is, given that the utility function of an investment is expressed as

$$U = E(r) - \frac{1}{2}A\sigma^2$$

where A is the measure of risk aversion, then the sign of A is irrelevant if the variance is zero (like that of a risk-free asset).
18. C is correct. The most risk-averse investor has the indifference curve with the greatest slope.
19. A is correct. A negative value in the given utility function indicates that the investor is a risk seeker.
20. C is correct. Investment 3 has the highest rate of return. Risk is irrelevant to a risk-neutral investor, who would have a measure of risk aversion equal to 0. Given the utility function, the risk neutral investor would obtain the greatest amount of utility from investment 3.

Investment	Expected Return	Expected Standard Deviation	Utility A = 0
1	18%	2%	0.1800
2	19%	8%	0.1900
3	20%	15%	0.2000
4	18%	30%	0.1800

21. C is correct. Investment 4 provides the highest utility value (0.2700) for a risk-seeking investor, who has a measure of risk aversion equal to –2.

Investment	Expected Return	Expected Standard Deviation	Utility A = −2
1	18%	2%	0.1804
2	19%	8%	0.1964
3	20%	15%	0.2225
4	18%	30%	0.2700

22. B is correct. Investment 2 provides the highest utility value (0.1836) for a risk-averse investor who has a measure of risk aversion equal to 2.

Investment	Expected Return	Expected Standard Deviation	Utility A = 2
1	18%	2%	0.1796
2	19%	8%	0.1836
3	20%	15%	0.1775
4	18%	30%	0.0900

23. A is correct. Investment 1 provides the highest utility value (0.1792) for a risk-averse investor who has a measure of risk aversion equal to 4.

Investment	Expected Return	Expected Standard Deviation	Utility A = 4
1	18%	2%	0.1792
2	19%	8%	0.1772
3	20%	15%	0.1550
4	18%	30%	0.0000

24. A is correct. The CAL is the combination of the risk-free asset with zero risk and the portfolio of all risky assets that provides for the set of feasible investments. Allowing for borrowing at the risk-free rate and investing in the portfolio of all risky assets provides for attainable portfolios that dominate risky assets below the CAL.
25. B is correct. The CAL represents the set of all feasible investments. Each investor's indifference curve determines the optimal combination of the risk-free asset and the portfolio of all risky assets, which must lie on the CAL.
26. C is correct.

$R_p = w_1 \times R_1 + (1 - w_1) \times R_2$

$R_p = w_1 \times 16\% + (1 - w_1) \times 12\%$

$15\% = 0.75(16\%) + 0.25(12\%)$.

27. A is correct.

$$\begin{aligned}\sigma_{port} &= \sqrt{w_1^2\sigma_1^2 + w_2^2\sigma_2^2 + 2w_1w_2\rho_{1,2}\sigma_1\sigma_2} \\ &= \sqrt{(0.5)^2(20\%)^2 + (0.5)^2(20\%)^2 + 2(0.5)(0.5)(-0.15)(20\%)(20\%)} \\ &= (1.0000\% + 1.0000\% - 0.3000\%)^{0.5} = (1.7000\%)^{0.5} = 13.04\%.\end{aligned}$$

28. B is correct.

$$\begin{aligned}\sigma_{port} &= \sqrt{w_1^2\sigma_1^2 + w_2^2\sigma_2^2 + 2w_1w_2\rho_{1,2}\sigma_1\sigma_2} \\ &= \sqrt{(0.5)^2(20\%)^2 + (0.5)^2(20\%)^2 + 2(0.5)(0.5)(0.00)(20\%)(20\%)} \\ &= (1.0000\% + 1.0000\% + 0.0000\%)^{0.5} = (2.0000\%)^{0.5} = 14.14\%.\end{aligned}$$

29. B is correct. The contribution of each individual asset's variance (or standard deviation) to the portfolio's volatility decreases as the number of assets in the equally weighted portfolio increases. The contribution of the co-movement measures between the assets increases (i.e., covariance and correlation) as the number of assets in the equally weighted

portfolio increases. The following equation for the variance of an equally weighted portfolio illustrates these points:

$$\sigma_p^2 = \frac{\bar{\sigma}^2}{N} + \frac{N-1}{N}\overline{COV} = \frac{\bar{\sigma}^2}{N} + \frac{N-1}{N}\bar{\rho}\bar{\sigma}^2$$

30. C is correct. The co-movement measures between the assets increases (i.e., covariance and correlation) as the number of assets in the equally weighted portfolio increases. The contribution of each individual asset's variance (or standard deviation) to the portfolio's volatility decreases as the number of assets in the equally weighted portfolio increases. The following equation for the variance of an equally weighted portfolio illustrates these points:

$$\sigma_p^2 = \frac{\bar{\sigma}^2}{N} + \frac{N-1}{N}\overline{COV} = \frac{\bar{\sigma}^2}{N} + \frac{N-1}{N}\bar{\rho}\bar{\sigma}^2$$

31. A is correct. Higher correlations will produce less diversification benefits provided that the other components of the portfolio standard deviation do not change (i.e., the weights and standard deviations of the individual assets).
32. C is correct. Asset 2 and Asset 3 have returns that are the same for Outcome 2, but the exact opposite returns for Outcome 1 and Outcome 3; therefore, because they move in opposite directions at the same magnitude, they are perfectly negatively correlated.
33. C is correct. An equally weighted portfolio of Asset 2 and Asset 3 will have the lowest portfolio standard deviation, because for each outcome the portfolio has the same expected return (they are perfectly negatively correlated).
34. A is correct. An equally weighted portfolio of Asset 1 and Asset 2 has the highest level of volatility of the three pairs. All three pairs have the same expected return; however, the portfolio of Asset 1 and Asset 2 provides the least amount of risk reduction.
35. C is correct. The minimum-variance frontier does not account for the risk-free rate. The minimum-variance frontier is the set of all attainable risky assets with the highest expected return for a given level of risk or the lowest amount of risk for a given level of return.
36. C is correct. The global minimum-variance portfolio is the portfolio on the minimum-variance frontier with the lowest standard deviation. Although the portfolio is attainable, when the risk-free asset is considered, the global minimum-variance portfolio is not the optimal risky portfolio.
37. B is correct. The Markowitz efficient frontier has higher rates of return for a given level of risk. With respect to the minimum-variance portfolio, the Markowitz efficient frontier is the set of portfolios above the global minimum-variance portfolio that dominates the portfolios below the global minimum-variance portfolio.
38. A is correct. The use of leverage and the combination of a risk-free asset and the optimal risky asset will dominate the efficient frontier of risky assets (the Markowitz efficient frontier).
39. B is correct. The CAL dominates the efficient frontier at all points except for the optimal risky portfolio. The ability of the investor to purchase additional amounts of the optimal risky portfolio by borrowing (i.e., buying on margin) at the risk-free rate makes higher rates of return for levels of risk greater than the optimal risky asset possible.
40. C is correct. Each individual investor's optimal mix of the risk-free asset and the optimal risky asset is determined by the investor's risk preference.

CHAPTER 6

PORTFOLIO RISK AND RETURN: PART II

SOLUTIONS

1. B is correct. The capital allocation line, CAL, is a combination of the risk-free asset and a risky asset (or a portfolio of risky assets). The combination of the risk-free asset and the market portfolio is a special case of the CAL, which is the capital market line, CML.
2. B is correct. A portfolio of the risk-free asset and a risky asset or a portfolio of risky assets can result in a better risk-return tradeoff than an investment in only one type of an asset, because the risk-free asset has zero correlation with the risky asset.
3. B is correct. Investors will have different optimal portfolios depending on their indifference curves. The optimal portfolio for each investor is the one with highest utility; that is, where the CAL is tangent to the individual investor's highest possible indifference curve.
4. B is correct. Although the optimal risky portfolio is the market portfolio, highly risk-averse investors choose to invest most of their wealth in the risk-free asset.
5. B is correct. Although the capital allocation line includes all possible combinations of the risk-free asset and any risky portfolio, the capital market line is a special case of the capital allocation line, which uses the market portfolio as the optimal risky portfolio.
6. A is correct. The market includes all risky assets, or anything that has value; however, not all assets are tradable, and not all tradable assets are investable.
7. A is correct. The optimal risky portfolio is the market portfolio. Capital market theory assumes that investors have homogeneous expectations, which means that all investors analyze securities in the same way and are rational. That is, investors use the same probability distributions, use the same inputs for future cash flows, and arrive at the same valuations. Because their valuations of all assets are identical, all investors will invest in the same optimal risky portfolio (i.e., the market portfolio).
8. C is correct. Theoretically, any point above the CML is not achievable and any point below the CML is dominated by and inferior to any point on the CML.
9. B is correct. As one moves further to the right of point M on the capital market line, an increasing amount of borrowed money is being invested in the market portfolio. This means that there is negative investment in the risk-free asset, which is referred to as a leveraged position in the risky portfolio.

10. A is correct. The combinations of the risk-free asset and the market portfolio on the CML where returns are less than the returns on the market portfolio are termed "lending" portfolios.
11. C is correct. Investors are capable of avoiding nonsystematic risk by forming a portfolio of assets that are not highly correlated with one another, thereby reducing total risk and being exposed only to systematic risk.
12. B is correct. Nonsystematic risk is specific to a firm, whereas systematic risk affects the entire economy.
13. B is correct. Only systematic risk is priced. Investors do not receive any return for accepting nonsystematic or diversifiable risk.
14. C is correct. The sum of systematic variance and nonsystematic variance equals the total variance of the asset. References to total risk as the sum of systematic risk and nonsystematic risk refer to variance, not to risk.
15. B is correct. In the market model, $R_i = \alpha_i + \beta_i R_m + e_i$, the intercept, αi, and slope coefficient, βi, are estimated using historical security and market returns.
16. B is correct. In the market model, $R_i = \alpha_i + \beta_i R_m + e_i$, the slope coefficient, βi, is an estimate of the asset's systematic or market risk.
17. A is correct. In the market model, $R_i = \alpha_i + \beta_i R_m + e_i$, the intercept, αi, and slope coefficient, βi, are estimated using historical security and market returns. These parameter estimates then are used to predict firm-specific returns that a security may earn in a future period.
18. A is correct. Security 1 has the highest total variance; $0.0625 = 0.25^2$ compared to Security 2 and Security 3 with a total variance of 0.0400.
19. C is correct. Security 3 has the highest beta value;

$$1.60 = \frac{\rho_{3,m}\sigma_3}{\sigma_m} = \frac{(0.80)(20\%)}{10\%}$$

compared to Security 1 and Security 2 with beta values of 1.50 and 1.40, respectively.
20. B is correct. Security 2 has the lowest beta value;

$$1.40 = \frac{\rho_{2,m}\sigma_2}{\sigma_m} = \frac{(0.70)(20\%)}{10\%}$$

compared to Security 1 and 3 with beta values of 1.50 and 1.60, respectively.
21. B is correct. The average beta of all assets in the market, by definition, is equal to 1.0.
22. A is correct. The security characteristic line is a plot of the excess return of the security on the excess return of the market. In such a graph, Jensen's alpha is the intercept and the beta is the slope.
23. B is correct. The security market line (SML) is a graphical representation of the capital asset pricing model, with beta risk on the x-axis and expected return on the y-axis.
24. B is correct. The security market line applies to any security, efficient or not. The CAL and the CML use the total risk of the asset (or portfolio of assets) rather than its systematic risk, which is the only risk that is priced.
25. A is correct. The CAPM shows that the primary determinant of expected return for an individual asset is its beta, or how well the asset correlates with the market.
26. A is correct. If an asset's beta is negative, the required return will be less than the risk-free rate in the CAPM. When combined with a positive market return, the asset reduces the

risk of the overall portfolio, which makes the asset very valuable. Insurance is an example of a negative beta asset.

27. B is correct. In the CAPM, the market risk premium is the difference between the return on the market and the risk-free rate, which is the same as the return in excess of the market return.
28. B is correct. The expected return of Security 1, using the CAPM, is 12.0% = 3% + 1.5 (6%); $E(R_i) = R_f + \beta_i(E(R_m) - R_f)$.
29. B is correct. The expected risk premium for Security 2 is 8.4% (11.4% − 3%), which indicates that the expected market risk premium is 6%; therefore, since the risk-free rate is 3% the expected rate of return for the market is 9%. That is, using the CAPM, $E(R_i) = R_f + \beta_i(E(R_m) - R_f)$, 11.4% = 3% + 1.4(X%), where X% = (11.4% − 3%)/1.4 = 6.0% = market risk premium.
30. C is correct. Security 3 has the highest beta; thus, regardless of the value for the risk-free rate, Security 3 will have the highest expected return; $E(R_i) = R_f + \beta_i(E(R_m) - R_f)$.
31. C is correct. Security 3 has the highest beta; thus, regardless of the risk-free rate, the expected return of Security 3 will be most sensitive to a change in the expected market return.
32. C is correct. Jensen's alpha adjusts for systematic risk, and *M*-squared and the Sharpe Ratio adjust for total risk.
33. C is correct. The sign of Jensen's alpha indicates whether or not the portfolio has outperformed the market. If alpha is positive, the portfolio has outperformed the market; if alpha is negative, the portfolio has underperformed the market.
34. A is correct. *M*-squared adjusts for risk using standard deviation (i.e., total risk).
35. B is correct. If the estimated return of an asset is above the SML (the expected return), the asset has a lower level of risk relative to the amount of expected return and would be a good choice for investment (i.e., undervalued).
36. A is correct. The homogeneity assumption refers to all investors having the same economic expectation of future cash flows. If all investors have the same expectations, then all investors should invest in the same optimal risky portfolio, therefore implying the existence of only one optimal portfolio (i.e., the market portfolio).
37. B is correct. The homogeneous expectations assumption means that all investors analyze securities in the same way and are rational. That is, they use the same probability distributions, use the same inputs for future cash flows, and arrive at the same valuations. Because their valuation of all assets is identical, they will generate the same optimal risky portfolio, which is the market portfolio.
38. C is correct. This is because of the plot of the excess return of the security on the excess return of the market. In such a graph, Jensen's alpha is the intercept and the beta is the slope.
39. C is correct. Since managers are concerned with maximizing risk-adjusted returns, securities with a higher value of Jensen's alpha, αi, should have a higher weight.
40. C is correct. Since managers are concerned with maximizing risk-adjusted returns, securities with greater nonsystematic risk should be given less weight in the portfolio.

CHAPTER 7

BASICS OF PORTFOLIO PLANNING AND CONSTRUCTION

SOLUTIONS

1. C is correct. Depending on circumstances, a written IPS or its equivalent may be required by law or regulation and a written IPS is certainly consistent with best practices. The mere fact that a written IPS is prepared for a client, however, does not *ensure* that risk and return objectives will in fact be achieved.
2. A is correct. A written IPS is best seen as a communication instrument allowing clients and portfolio managers to mutually establish investment objectives and constraints.
3. B is correct. A written IPS, to be successful, must incorporate a full understanding of the client's situation and requirements. As stated in the reading, "The IPS will be developed following a fact-finding discussion with the client."
4. B is correct. The major components of an IPS are listed in Section 2.2 of the reading. Investment Guidelines are described as the section that provides information about how policy may be executed, including investment constraints. The Statement of Duties and Responsibilities "detail[s] the duties and responsibilities of the client, the custodian of the client's assets, the investment managers, and so forth." Investment Objectives is "a section explaining the client's objectives in investing."
5. C is correct. The major components of an IPS are listed in Section 2.2 of the reading. Strategic Asset Allocation (also known as the policy portfolio) and Rebalancing Policy are often included as appendices to the IPS. The Statement of Duties and Responsibilities, however, is an integral part of the IPS and is unlikely to be placed in an appendix.
6. B is correct. According to the reading, "The sections of an IPS that are most closely linked to the client's distinctive needs are those dealing with investment objectives and constraints." Investment Guidelines "[provide] information about how policy may be executed, including investment constraints." The section titled Procedures "[details] the steps to be taken to keep the IPS current and the procedures to follow to respond to various contingencies." The Statement of Duties and Responsibilities "detail[s] the duties and responsibilities of the client, the custodian of the client's assets, the investment managers, and so forth."

7. A is correct. Because the return objective specifies a target return *relative to* the FTSE 100 Index, the objective is best described as a relative return objective.
8. C is correct. Risk attitude is a subjective factor and measuring risk attitude is difficult. Oftentimes, investment managers use psychometric questionnaires, such as those developed by Grable and Joo (2004), to assess a client's willingness to take risk.
9. B is correct. The reference to the DAX marks this response as a relative risk objective. Value at risk establishes a maximum value of loss expected during a specified time period at a given level of probability. A statement of maximum allowed absolute loss (€2.5 million) is an absolute risk objective.
10. C is correct. Measuring willingness to take risk (risk tolerance, risk aversion) is an exercise in applied psychology. Instruments attempting to measure risk attitudes exist, but they are clearly less objective than measurements of ability to take risk. Ability to take risk is based on relatively objective traits such as expected income, time horizon, and existing wealth relative to liabilities.
11. A is correct. The volatility of the client's income and the significant support needs for his mother and himself suggest that the client has a low ability to take risk. The client's trading experience and his responses to the risk assessment questionnaire indicate that the client has an above-average willingness to take risk.
12. B is correct. On the one hand, the client has a stable, high income and no dependents. On the other hand, she exhibits above-average risk aversion. Her ability to take risk is high, but her willingness to take risk is low.
13. A is correct. The client's financial objectives are long term. Her stable employment indicates that her immediate liquidity needs are modest. The children will not go to college until 10 or more years later. Her time horizon is best described as being long term.
14. B is correct. The unpredictable nature of property and casualty (P&C) claims forces P&C insurers to allocate a substantial proportion of their investments into liquid, short maturity assets. This need for liquidity also forces P&C companies to accept investments with relatively low expected returns. Liquidity is of less concern to life insurance companies given the greater predictability of life insurance payouts.
15. B is correct. When a client has a restriction in trading, such as this obligation to refrain from trading, the IPS "should note this constraint so that the portfolio manager does not inadvertently trade the stock on the client's behalf."
16. A is correct. The correlation between U.S. equities and Brazilian equities is 0.76. The correlations between U.S. equities and East Asian equities and the correlation between U.S. equities and European equities both exceed 0.76. Lower correlations indicate a greater degree of separation between asset classes. Therefore, using solely the data given in the table, returns on Brazilian equities are most sharply distinguished from returns on U.S. equities.
17. C is correct. Strategic asset allocation depends on several principles. As stated in the reading, "One principle is that a portfolio's systematic risk accounts for most of its change in value over the long run." A second principle is that "the returns to groups of like assets . . . predictably reflect exposures to certain sets of systematic factors." This latter principle establishes that returns on asset classes primarily reflect the systematic risks of the classes.
18. C is correct. As the reading states, "an asset class should contain homogeneous assets . . . paired correlations of securities would be high within an asset class, but should be lower versus securities in other asset classes."

19. B is correct. Tactical asset allocation allows actual asset allocation to deviate from that of the strategic asset allocation (policy portfolio) of the IPS. Tactical asset allocation attempts to take advantage of temporary dislocations from the market conditions and assumptions that drove the policy portfolio decision.
20. A is correct. The core–satellite approach to constructing portfolios is defined as "investing the majority of the portfolio on a passive or low active risk basis while a minority of the assets is managed aggressively in smaller portfolios."

CHAPTER 8

OVERVIEW OF EQUITY SECURITIES

SOLUTIONS

1. C is correct. The company is not obligated to make dividend payments. It is at the discretion of the company whether or not it chooses to pay dividends.
2. B is correct. Statutory voting is the type of equity voting right that grants one vote per share owned.
3. A is correct. Preference shares do not have to be either callable or putable.
4. C is correct. Participating preference shares entitle shareholders to receive an additional dividend if the company's profits exceed a predetermined level.
5. B is correct. Private equity securities do not have market-determined quoted prices.
6. C is correct. Venture capital investments can be used to provide mezzanine financing to companies in their early stage of development.
7. B is correct. Regulatory and investor relations costs are lower for private equity firms than for public firms. There are no stock exchange, regulatory, or shareholder involvements with private equity, whereas for public firms these costs can be high.
8. C is correct. The trends in emerging markets have not led to the stability of foreign exchange markets.
9. A is correct. In an unsponsored DR, the depository bank owns the voting rights to the shares. The bank purchases the shares, places them into a trust, and then sells shares in the trust—not the underlying shares—in other markets.
10. A is correct. The listing fees on Level III sponsored ADRs are high.
11. C is correct. An ETF is used to gain exposure to a basket of securities (equity, fixed income, commodity futures, etc.).
12. A is correct. The formula states $R_t = (P_t - P_{t-1} + D_t)/P_t$. Therefore, total return $= (42 - 50 + 2)/50 = -12.0\%$.
13. A is correct. The depreciated value of the euro will create an additional loss in the form of currency return that is lower than the ETF's return.
14. C is correct. Some equity securities do not pay dividends, and therefore the standard deviation of dividends cannot be used to measure the risk of all equity securities.
15. A is correct. Putable shares, whether common or preference, give the investor the option to sell the shares back to the issuer at a predetermined price. This predetermined price

creates a floor for the share's price that reduces the uncertainty of future cash flows for the investor (i.e., lowers risk relative to the other two types of shares listed).

16. C is correct. Issuing shares in the primary (and secondary) market *reduces* a company's return on equity because it increases the total amount of equity capital invested in the company (i.e., the denominator in the ROE formula).
17. C is correct. Capital is raised to ensure the company's existence only when it is required. It is not a typical goal of raising capital.
18. A is correct. A company's book value increases when a company retains its net income.
19. A is correct. The book value of the company is equal to total assets minus total liabilities, which is €12,000,000 − €7,500,000 = €4,500,000.
20. A is correct. A company's market value is affected by management's decisions. Management's decisions can directly affect the company's *book* value, which can then affect its market value.
21. B is correct. A company's ROE is calculated as (NI_t/BVE_{t-1}). For 2009, the BVE_{t-1} is equal to the beginning total assets minus the beginning total liabilities, which equals £50,000,000 − £35,000,000 = £15,000,000. Therefore, ROE_{2009} = £2,000,000/£15,000,000 = 13.3%.
22. C is correct. A company's ROE will increase if it issues debt to repurchase outstanding shares of equity.
23. B is correct. The cost of equity is not easily determined. It is dependent on investors' required rate of return on equity, which reflects the different risk levels of investors and their expectations about the company's future cash flows.
24. B is correct. Companies try to raise funds at the lowest possible cost. Therefore, cost of equity is used as a proxy for the minimum required rate of return.

CHAPTER 9

INTRODUCTION TO INDUSTRY AND COMPANY ANALYSIS

SOLUTIONS

1. C is correct. Tactical asset allocation involves timing investments in asset classes and does not make use of industry analysis.
2. C is correct. A sector rotation strategy is conducted by investors wishing to time investment in industries through an analysis of fundamentals and/or business-cycle conditions.
3. B is correct. Determination of a company's competitive environment depends on understanding its industry.
4. A is correct. The Russell system uses three tiers, whereas the other two systems are based on four tiers or levels.
5. B is correct. Personal care products are classified as consumer staples in the "Description of Representative Sectors."
6. C is correct. Commercial systems are generally updated more frequently than government systems, and include only publicly traded for-profit companies.
7. B is correct. Business-cycle sensitivity falls on a continuum and is not a discrete "either–or" phenomenon.
8. C is correct. Customers' flexibility as to when they purchase the product makes the product more sensitive to the business cycle.
9. C is correct. Varying conditions of recession or expansion around the world would affect the comparisons of companies with sales in different regions of the world.
10. B is correct. Constructing a peer group is a subjective process, and a logical starting point is to begin with a commercially available classification system. This system will identify a group of companies that may have properties comparable to the business activity of interest.
11. A is correct because it is a false statement. Reviewing the annual report to find management's discussion about the competitive environment and specific competitors is a suggested step in the process of constructing a peer group.
12. B is correct. The company could be in more than one peer group depending on the demand drivers for the business segments, although the multiple business segments may make it difficult to classify the company.

13. C is correct. For the automobile industry, the high capital requirements and other elements mentioned in the reading provide high barriers to entry, and recognition that auto factories are generally only of use for manufacturing cars implies a high barrier to exit.
14. C is correct. A slow pace of product innovation often means that customers prefer to stay with suppliers they know, implying stable market shares.
15. C is correct. Capacity increases in providing legal services would not involve several factors that would be important to the other two industries, including the need for substantial fixed capital investments or, in the case of a restaurant, outfitting rental or purchased space. These requirements would tend to slow down, respectively, steel production and restaurant expansion.
16. B is correct. Vision typically deteriorates at advanced ages. An increased number of older adults implies that more eyewear products will be purchased.
17. B is correct. As their educational level increases, workers are able to perform more skilled tasks and earn higher wages and, as a result, have more income left for discretionary expenditures.
18. A is correct. Seeking economies of scale would tend to reduce per-unit costs and increase profit.
19. C is correct. The embryonic stage is characterized by slow growth and high prices.
20. C is correct. The growth phase is not likely to experience price wars because expanding industry demand provides companies the opportunity to grow even without increasing market share. When industry growth is stagnant, companies may be able to grow only by increasing market share, for example, by engaging in price competition.
21. B is correct.
22. C is correct. The relatively few members of the industry generally try to avoid price competition.
23. C is correct. With short lead times, industry capacity can be rapidly increased to satisfy demand, but it may also lead to overcapacity and lower profits.
24. A is correct. An industry that has high barriers to entry generally requires substantial physical capital and/or financial investment. With weak pricing power in the industry, finding a buyer for excess capacity (i.e., to exit the industry) may be difficult.
25. C is correct. Economic profit is earned and value created for shareholders when the company earns returns above the company's cost of capital.
26. C is correct. Although the threat of government intervention may be considered an element of some of Porter's five forces, it is not one of the listed forces.
27. B is correct. As displayed in Exhibit 9–4, the alcoholic beverage industry is concentrated and possesses strong pricing power.
28. A is correct. The oil services industry has medium barriers to entry because a company with a high level of technological innovation could obtain a niche market in a specific area of expertise.
29. A is correct. Companies with low cost strategies must be able to invest in productivity-improving equipment and finance that investment at a low cost of capital. Market share and pricing depend on whether the strategy is pursued defensively or offensively.
30. A is correct. The cost structure is an appropriate element when analyzing the supply of the product, but analysis of demand relies on the product's differentiating characteristics and the customers' needs and wants.
31. C is correct. The corporate profile would provide an understanding of these elements.

CHAPTER 10

EQUITY VALUATION: CONCEPTS AND BASIC TOOLS

SOLUTIONS

1. A is correct. The current market price of the stock exceeds the upper bound of the analyst's estimate of the intrinsic value of the stock.
2. A is correct. The market price is less than the estimated intrinsic, or fundamental, value.
3. C is correct. Asset-based valuation models calculate the intrinsic value of equity by subtracting liabilities from the market value of assets.
4. C is correct. It is a form of present value, or discounted cash flow, model. Both enterprise value (EV) and free cash flow to equity (FCFE) are forms of multiplier models.
5. C is correct. Multiplier valuation models (in the form of P/B) and asset-based valuation models (in the form of adjustments to book value) use book value, whereas present value models typically discount future expected cash flows.
6. B is correct. To use a discounted cash flow model, the analyst will require FCFE or dividend data. In addition, the analyst will need data to calculate an appropriate discount rate.
7. B is correct. The FCFE model assumes that dividend-paying capacity is reflected in FCFE.
8. C is correct. According to the dividend discount model, the intrinsic value of a stock today is the present value of all future dividends. In this case, the intrinsic value is the present value of D_1, D_2, and P_2. Note that P_2 is the present value at Period 2 of all future dividends from Period 3 to infinity.
9. A is correct. In the FCFE model, the intrinsic value of stock is calculated by discounting expected future FCFE to present value. No further adjustments are required.
10. C is correct. Dividend discount models can be used for a stock that pays a current dividend or a stock that is expected to pay a dividend. FCFE can be used for both of those stocks and for stocks that do not, or are not expected to, pay dividends in the near future. Both of these models are forms of present-value models.
11. B is correct. The expected annual dividend is 4.80% × \$25 = \$1.20. The value of a preferred share is \$1.20/0.0449 = \$26.73.

12. B is correct. The required rate of return, r, can vary widely depending on the inputs and is not unique. A preferred stock with a constant dividend would not have a growth rate to estimate, and the investor's time horizon would have no effect on the calculation of intrinsic value.
13. C is correct. $P_0 = D_1/(r - g) = 1.75(1.092)/(0.123 - 0.092) = \$61.65$.
14. C is correct. According to the Gordon growth model, $V_0 = D_1/(r - g)$. In this case, $D_1 = \$2.00 \times 1.04 = \$2.08$, so $V_0 = \$2.08/(0.07 - 0.04) = \$69.3333 = \$69.33$.
15. A is correct. The current price of €22.56 is less than the intrinsic value (V_0) of €24.64; therefore, the stock appears to be currently undervalued. According to the two-stage dividend discount model:

$$V_0=\sum_{t=1}^{n}\frac{D_0(1+g_S)^t}{(1+r)^t}+\frac{V_n}{(1+r)^n} \quad \text{and} \quad V_n=\frac{D_{n+1}}{r-g_L}$$

$$D_{n+1}=D_0(1+g_S)^n(1+g_L)$$

$D_1 = €1.60 \times 1.09 = €1.744$
$D_2 = €1.60 \times (1.09)^2 = €1.901$
$D_3 = €1.60 \times (1.09)^3 = €2.072$
$D_4 = €1.60 \times (1.09)^4 = €2.259$
$D_5 = [€1.60 \times (1.09)^4](1.04) = €2.349$
$V_4 = €2.349/(0.12 - 0.04) = €29.363$

$$V_0 = \frac{1.744}{(1.12)^1}+\frac{1.901}{(1.12)^2}+\frac{2.072}{(1.12)^3}+\frac{2.259}{(1.12)^4}+\frac{29.363}{(1.12)^4}$$

$$= 1.557 + 1.515 + 1.475 + 1.436 + 18.661$$

$= €24.64$ (which is greater than the current price of €22.56).

16. C is correct.

$$V_0 = \frac{D_1}{(1+r)}+\frac{D_2}{(1+r)^2}+\frac{P_2}{(1+r)^2}$$

$$= \frac{0.70}{(1.083)}+\frac{0.80}{(1.083)^2}+\frac{31.29}{(1.083)^2}$$

$$= \$28.01$$

Note that $D_1 = 0.58(1.20) = 0.70$, $D_2 = 0.58(1.20)(1.15) = 0.80$, and $P_2 = D_3/(k - g) = 0.80(1.056)/(0.083 - 0.056) = 31.29$

17. B is correct.

$$V_0 = \frac{D_1}{(1+r)}+\frac{D_2}{(1+r)^2}+\frac{D_3}{(1+r)^3}+\frac{D_4}{(1+r)^4}+\frac{P_4}{(1+r)^4}$$

$$= \frac{468}{(1.12)}+\frac{486.72}{(1.12)^2}+\frac{506.19}{(1.12)^3}+\frac{526.44}{(1.12)^4}+\frac{9000}{(1.12)^4}$$

$$= ¥7,220$$

18. B is correct. The Gordon growth model (also known as the constant growth model) can be used to value dividend-paying companies in a mature phase of growth. A stable dividend growth rate is often a plausible assumption for such companies.

19. C is correct. The Gordon growth model is best suited to valuing mature companies. The two-stage model is best for companies that are transitioning from a growth stage to a mature stage. The three-stage model is appropriate for young companies just entering the growth phase.
20. A is correct. The company is a mature company with a steadily growing dividend rate. The two-stage (or multistage) model is unnecessary because the dividend growth rate is expected to remain stable. Although an FCFE model could be used, that model is more often chosen for companies that currently pay no dividends.
21. C is correct. The justified forward P/E is calculated as follows:

$$\frac{P_0}{E_1} = \frac{\frac{D_1}{E_1}}{r-g}$$

P/E is inversely related to the required rate of return, r, and directly related to the growth rate, g, and the dividend payout ratio, D/E.
22. A is correct. Multiples based on comparables are grounded in the law of one price and take into account historical multiple values. In contrast, P/E multiples based on fundamentals can be based on the Gordon growth model, which takes into account future expected dividends.
23. A is correct. The statement is inaccurate in both respects. Although multiples can be calculated from historical data, forecasted values can be used as well. For companies without accounting earnings, several other multiples can be used. These multiples are often specific to a company's industry or sector and include price-to-sales and price-to-cash flow.
24. A is correct. Tanaka shares are most likely overvalued. As the table below shows, all the 2009 multiples are currently above their 2005–2008 averages.

Year	P/E	P/CF	P/R
2005	4.9	5.4	1.2
2006	6.1	8.6	1.5
2007	8.3	7.3	1.9
2008	9.2	7.9	2.3
Average	7.1	7.3	1.7

25. B is correct.

$$\frac{P_0}{E_1} = \frac{\frac{D_1}{E_1}}{r-g} = \frac{\frac{2.7}{5.7}}{0.0835-0.0275} = 8.5$$

26. B is correct. P/E = Current price/EPS, and Estimated P/E = Current price/Estimated EPS.
    Alpha P/E = \$57.32/\$3.82 = 15.01
    Alpha estimated P/E = \$57.32/4.75 = 12.07
    Delta P/E = \$18.93/\$1.35 = 14.02
    Delta estimated P/E = \$18.93/\$1.40 = 13.52
27. C is correct. Relative to the others, Pioneer Trust has the lowest P/E multiple and the P/B multiple is tied for the lowest with Prime Bank. Given the law of one price, similar

companies should trade at similar P/B and P/E levels. Thus, based on the information presented, Pioneer is most likely to be undervalued.

28. C is correct. Enterprise value is calculated as the market value of equity plus the market value of debt and preferred stock minus short-term investments. Therefore, the market value of equity is enterprise value minus the market value of debt and preferred stock plus short-term investments.
29. A is correct. Operating income may be used in place of EBITDA when calculating the enterprise value multiple. EBITDA may be used when company earnings are negative because EBITDA is usually positive. The book value of debt cannot be used in place of market value of debt.
30. A is correct.
    $EV = 10.2 \times 22{,}000{,}000 = \$224{,}400{,}000$

$$\begin{aligned}\text{Equity value} &= \text{EV} - \text{Debt} + \text{Cash} = 224{,}400{,}000 - 56{,}000{,}000 + 1{,}500{,}000\\ &= \$169{,}900{,}000\end{aligned}$$

31. B is correct. The market value of debt must be calculated and taken out of the enterprise value. Enterprise value, sometimes known as the cost of a takeover, is the cost of the purchase of the company, which would include the assumption of the company's debts at market value.
32. B is correct. Intangible assets are hard to value. Therefore, asset-based valuation models work best for companies that do not have a high proportion of intangible assets.
33. A is correct. Asset-based valuations are most often used when an analyst is valuing private enterprises. Both B and C are considerations in asset-based valuations but are more likely to be reasons to avoid that valuation model rather than reasons to use it.
34. B is correct. According to the reading, analysts may not have access to market quotations for company debt.
35. A is correct. Although all models can be used to compare various companies, multiplier models have the advantage of reducing varying fundamental data points into a format that allows direct comparisons. As long as the analyst applies the data in a consistent manner for all the companies, this approach provides useful comparative data.
36. B is correct. Very small changes in inputs, such as required rate of return or dividend growth rate, can result in large changes to the valuation model output. Some present-value models, such as FCFE models, can be used to value companies without dividends. Also, the intrinsic value of a security is independent of the investor's holding period.

CHAPTER 11

EQUITY MARKET VALUATION

SOLUTIONS

1. A. Using the Gordon growth model we have:

$$V_0 = \frac{D_0(1+g)}{r-g}$$

Here $D_0 = 450$
$g = 5.5\%$
$r = 7.5\%$

so that:

$$V_0 = \frac{450(1+0.055)}{0.075-0.055} = 23{,}738$$

B. One variable needed in the H-model is the initial growth rate of the dividend, and another is the number of years during which the dividend growth rate declines from its initial value to the long-term sustainable growth rate. In contrast, such a variable is not present in the Gordon growth model because a single dividend rate applies from the date of valuation to perpetuity.

C. The Fed model predicts that stocks are overvalued if the forward earnings yield on the equity index (here 6 percent) is less than the yield on Treasury bonds (here 7 percent). Therefore, in Emerge Country, stocks are overvalued.

The Fed model has three important limitations. It:

- Ignores the equity risk premium.
- Ignores earnings growth.
- Compares a real variable to a nominal variable.

D. Industry analysis fits in the middle of both top-down approach and bottom-up approach.

In the top-down approach, when entering industry analysis, the market analysis has already been completed, so that the analyst knows which equity markets will outperform (compared to bonds or real estate, for example). So what remains to be done is to determine the equity market sectors that are expected to be top performers in each of the already identified best-performing equity markets.

In the bottom-up approach, when entering industry analysis, the company analysis has already been completed, so the analyst knows which individual securities will outperform. What remains to be done is to aggregate the expected returns of those securities within each industry to identify the industries that are expected to be the best performers.

2. A. Using Equation 3, we have:

$$\begin{aligned}\text{Percentage growth in GDP} &= \text{growth in total factor productivity}\\ &+ (\text{output of elasticity of capital}) \times (\text{growth in capital stock})\\ &+ (1 - \text{output of elasticity of capital}) \times (\text{growth in labor input})\\ &= 0.6\% + (0.3 \times 3.5\%) + (0.7 \times 0.4\%)\\ &= 1.93\%\end{aligned}$$

B. *Measure 1:* Lowering the retirement age will reduce the growth in labor participation and therefore the growth in labor input until a new steady-state labor force participation rate is attained. Subsequent growth in labor input should then track underlying population growth.

Measure 2: Lowering the subsidies to higher education will most likely reduce future technical innovation and therefore reduce growth in total factor productivity. The effect may be slow at the beginning, but will increase gradually for a period that will extend well beyond the five years of reduction in subsidies.

C. Top-down and bottom-up forecasts frequently differ from each other. In these cases, the reconciling and revision process of the forecasts can:

- Help the analyst better understand the market consensus.
- Reveal a gap that gives rise to significant market opportunities.

In spite of the optimistic bias observed by Murray, the bottom-up approach (a) may provide the opportunity to identify attractively priced securities irrespective of the attractiveness of the sectors and (b) may be a better fit for the investors who focus on a market niche.

D. The denominators of the Tobin's *q* ratio and of the equity *q* ratio include the replacement cost of company assets. It is difficult to obtain those replacement costs for two reasons: (1) there may be no liquid markets for the assets, and (2) intangible assets are often difficult to value.

3. A is correct. It has been shown that bottom-up forecasts are often more optimistic than top-down forecasts (not the other way around). This may be because analysts rely on management's assessment of future probability.

4. C is correct. The contributions from total factor productivity are 2.5 percent and 2.8 percent, respectively, for the periods 1970–1989 and 1990–2009. The corresponding contributions from labor input are 1.8% (= 0.6 × 3.0%) and 2.76% (= 0.6 × 4.6%) and the corresponding contributions from capital stock are 1.92% (= 0.4 × 4.8%) and 1.76% (= 0.4 × 4.4%).

5. C is correct. Government-implemented measures are among the inputs that have an impact on the economy and therefore on the historical data that the analyst uses. It rests

upon the analyst to establish whether these measures will continue in the future when he or she projects economic growth.

6. A is correct. The Fed model, although developed in the United States, can be applied to the valuation of non-U.S. equity markets.
7. C is correct. The Yardeni model incorporates the effect on equity market value of long-term earnings growth.
8. B is correct. The P/10-year MA(E) model is dependent on changes in accounting rules because it averages earnings over 10 years. Therefore, the feature is not applicable to the model.
9. A is correct. The equity q ratio is equal to

$$\text{Market value of equities}/(\text{Replacement cost of assets} - \text{Liabilities})$$
$$= 9.0/(27.3 - 13.3)$$
$$= 0.6429$$

10. C is correct. A Tobin's q value of less than 1, when 1 is used as a comparison point, indicates that the company is undervalued in the marketplace because it indicates an opportunity to buy assets at a price below their replacement cost.
11. A is correct. It is true that the growth in total productivity is not directly observable. That growth is obtained by using the following data: growth in real output, growth in capital stock, and growth in labor input.
12. C is correct. A higher correlation of the U.S. equity market with international equity markets would increase the risk of the U.S. equity market and thus increase the required return (r) on that market. Increasing r would reduce the justified P/E ratio:

$$\frac{P_0}{E_1} = \frac{D_0(1+g)/E_1}{r-g}$$

13. A is correct. It would be true that the Fed model predicts that U.S. stocks are overvalued if the forward earnings yield on the S&P 500 (4.5 percent in this scenario 1) is less than the yield on U.S. Treasury bonds (4.75 percent in this scenario 1).
14. B is correct. A criticism of the Fed model that the Yardeni model does address is that the Fed model does not take account of long-term earnings growth. The Yardeni model includes a long-term earnings growth variable.
15. B is correct. The P/10-year MA(E) model is dependent on changes in accounting rules because it averages earnings over 10 years. Therefore, the feature is not applicable to the model.
16. C is correct. On the one hand, because the insurance company wants to minimize tracking errors with respect to the equity indexes, Carmichael should recommend the top-down approach because the forecast does not need to focus on individual security selection. On the other hand, because the insurance company wants to detect quickly any significant turn in equity markets, Carmichael should recommend the bottom-up approach because the bottom-up approach can be effective in anticipating cyclical turning points.

CHAPTER 12

TECHNICAL ANALYSIS

SOLUTIONS

1. A is correct. Almost all technical analysis relies on these data inputs.
2. A is correct. Technical analysis works because markets are *not* efficient and rational and because human beings tend to behave similarly in similar circumstances. The result is market trends and patterns that repeat themselves and are somewhat predictable.
3. A is correct. Trends generally must be in place for some time before they are recognizable. Thus, some time may be needed for a change in trend to be identified.
4. C is correct. Commodities and currencies do not have underlying financial statements or an income stream; thus, fundamental analysis is useless in determining theoretical values for them or whether they are over- or undervalued.
5. C is correct. The top and bottom of the bars indicate the highs and lows for the day; the line on the left indicates the opening price and the line on the right indicates the closing price.
6. C is correct. Dark and light shading is a unique feature of candlestick charts.
7. C is correct. Rising volume shows conviction by many market participants, which is likely to lead to a continuation of the trend.
8. A is correct. The price of gold in nominal dollars was several orders of magnitude cheaper 100 years ago than it is today (roughly US$20 then versus US$1,100 today). Such a wide range of prices lends itself well to being graphically displayed on a logarithmic scale.

9. B is correct. A downtrend line is constructed by drawing a line connecting the highs of the price chart.
10. B is correct. It is demonstrated in Exhibit A:

EXHIBIT A Candlestick Chart: GreatWall Information Industry Co., Ltd. Price Data, November 2008–September 2009 (price measured in RMB × 100)

11. B is correct.
12. C is correct. As shown in Exhibit B, Barclays shares traded up to 390p on three occasions each several weeks apart and declined thereafter each time.

EXHIBIT B Candlestick Chart: Barclays PLC Price Data, January 2009–January 2010 (price measured in British pence)

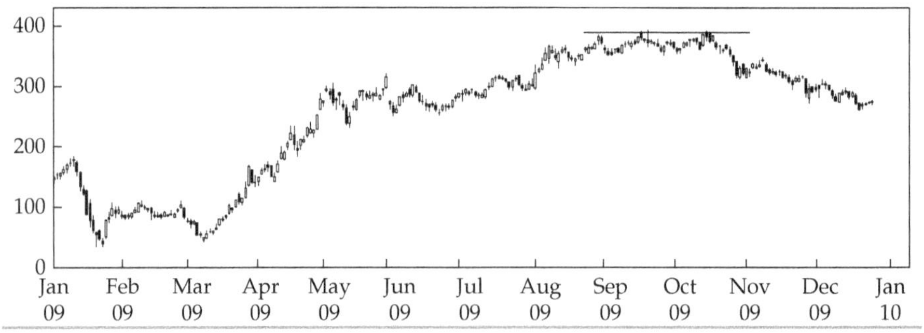

13. C is correct. The left shoulder formed at around US$18.50, the head formed at around US$20.50, and the second shoulder formed at around US$19, as shown in Exhibit C.

EXHIBIT C Candlestick Chart: Archer Daniels Midland Company, February 1996–February 2001

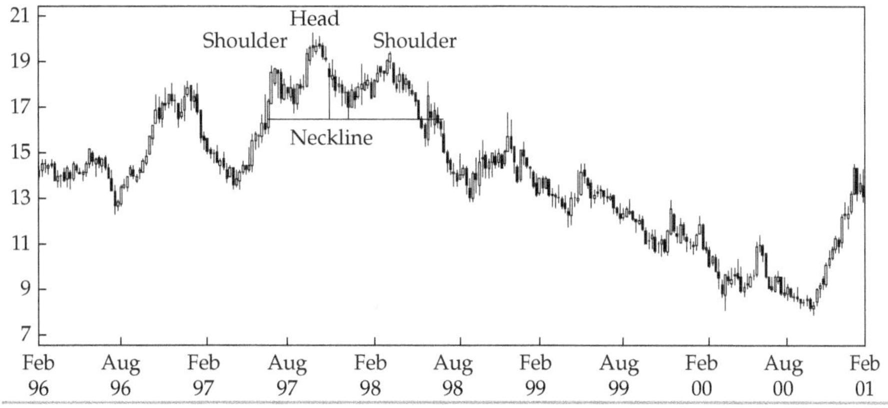

14. C is correct. Target = Neckline + (Neckline − Head): €100 + (€100 − €75) = €125.
15. A is correct. A large increase in the number of IPOs increases the supply of equity and, if overall demand remains the same, puts downward pressure on equities. Also, companies tend to issue shares of equity when the managers believe they will receive a premium price, which is also an indicator of a market top.
16. B is correct. A value below 1.0 is a bullish sign; it means more volume is in rising shares than in declining ones. The TRIN is calculated as: (Advancing issues/Declining issues)/(Volume of advancing issues/Volume of declining issues).
17. C is correct. Bollinger Bands consist of a moving average and a higher line representing the moving average plus a set number of standard deviations from average price (for the same number of periods as used to calculate the moving average) and a lower line that is a moving average minus the same number of standard deviations.
18. C is correct. Bollinger Bands are price-based indicators, *not* momentum oscillators, which are constructed so that they oscillate between a high and a low or around 0 or 100.
19. A is correct. Triangles are one of several continuation patterns.
20. C is correct. It is one of several reversal patterns.
21. A is correct. Volume is necessary to confirm the various market rallies and reversals during the formation of the head and shoulders pattern.
22. B is correct.
23. A is correct. The decennial pattern theory states that years ending with a 5 will have the best performance of any of the 10 years in a decade and that those ending with a zero will have the worst.
24. C is correct. A possible reason for the superior performance in the third year is that the U.S. presidential election occurs, together with a number of other elections, in a four-year cycle, so the politicians desiring to be reelected inject money into the economy in the third year to improve their chances of winning the following year.
25. A is correct. Long-term cycles require many years to complete; thus, not many cycles are available for observation.
26. B is correct.
27. A is correct. This is the term for a separate cycle theory.
28. C is correct. Relative strength analysis is often used to compare two asset classes or two securities.

ABOUT THE CFA PROGRAM

The Chartered Financial Analyst® designation (CFA®) is a globally recognized standard of excellence for measuring the competence and integrity of investment professionals. To earn the CFA charter, candidates must successfully pass through the CFA Program, a global graduate-level self-study program that combines a broad curriculum with professional conduct requirements as preparation for a wide range of investment specialties.

Anchored by a practice-based curriculum, the CFA Program is focused on the knowledge identified by professionals as essential to the investment decision-making process. This body of knowledge maintains current relevance through a regular, extensive survey of practicing CFA charterholders across the globe. The curriculum covers 10 general topic areas, ranging from equity and fixed-income analysis to portfolio management to corporate finance, all with a heavy emphasis on the application of ethics in professional practice. Known for its rigor and breadth, the CFA Program curriculum highlights principles common to every market so that professionals who earn the CFA designation have a thoroughly global investment perspective and a profound understanding of the global marketplace.

www.cfainstitute.org